# HOW TO STOP PROCRASTINATING

---

A PROVEN GUIDE TO OVERCOME
PROCRASTINATION, CURE LAZINESS &
PERFECTIONISM, USING SIMPLE 5-MINUTE
PRACTICES

CHASE HILL

SCOTT SHARP

# CONTENTS

# INTRODUCTION

Procrastinators seriously struggle with meeting deadlines, they feel like they aren't productive and generally don't enjoy crucial parts of their lives. If you are one of them, I know how you feel right now.

Nobody wants to be underproductive. If someone isn't achieving as much as they want to, it is mainly because of procrastination. The funny fact about procrastinators is that they already know they are procrastinating. I'm glad you are reading this. It is a sure sign that you want to overcome the problem of procrastination.

Trust me, once you have decided to do something about the problem, you've already taken the first step towards over-coming procrastination. If you spend some time and think about the concept of procrastination, you will understand that it has a lot to do with your productivity.

Imagine you are given a project to complete, if you finish it before the deadline, you'll be able to get another project. The amount you can potentially earn is directly related to how productive you can be. I know that saying it is just a case of increasing your productivity is an easy concept, but it doesn't have to be that difficult in reality.

Now that I have mentioned it, productivity doesn't imply working 24 hours a day. I'm definitely not encouraging continuous work. It's all about using the time you have available in the most productive way.

For example, if you have been given a week to complete a project, you must use it in the best way to get your work done. Instead, you may spend your time scrolling through Facebook feeds, Twitter, or any other social media account. Social media is one of the worst distractions for anyone, let alone a procrastinator. The words "I'll just check..." can turn 5 minutes into hours, hours that could be put towards meeting your deadline. One hour on the computer becomes 50% working and 50% seeing what others have done with their time. It becomes slightly ironic.

Plus, it wouldn't have been intentional, or you wouldn't even know that you are wasting time until you actually give it a thought.

Procrastination is more dangerous than many of us assume. However, there are always solutions to all problems. Even for procrastination, you have many practical solutions that can be put into place with perseverance and diligence.

There is no counter-argument whether or not procrastination kills your productivity, it just does!

For example, you are capable of achieving 90% of a task in a day. Due to procrastinating you'd only achieve 45%, which means you are significantly underproductive. When you are nearing the deadline, you might have to run a race to achieve your goal, and it will have a huge black spot on the quality.

But I would like to share something interesting; some people can produce high-quality work in a short time due to procrastinating. Yes, such people do exist, and we'll discuss their habits in this guide. If you don't like yourself being drawn to procrastination and if you don't want to be underproductive, you will benefit significantly from this book.

*«How to stop procrastinating»* will help you make time for the ones who actually need it. This book will help you overcome procrastination and to become a more productive individual!

Productive reading!

# CHAPTER 1: WHY YOU PROCRASTINATE. IDENTIFY YOUR ENEMY AND REASONS FOR SELF-SABOTAGE

Not everyone can do their work on time. Of course, there are people who complete their work on time, and we need such people. But we are talking about the other group who are struggling to make it on time. The ones who can't meet their task deadlines and are procrastinating regularly.

You've already discovered that you are procrastinating and now, you are looking for ways to overcome the problem. This is something great! A decision has been made.

If you are someone who hasn't yet understood the fact that you are delaying your work, then, it's something serious. But you are here because you have understood it. Now, let's discuss the concept of procrastination in-depth.

Why do you procrastinate? Is it because you aren't moti-vated or is it because you are bored with that particular work? Sometimes, procrastination is directly related to your mentality. And other times, it has nothing do with your behavior, but your mood. Likewise, there are different reasons for procrastination. We'll be discussing all the reasons that make an individual procrastinate.

Unfortunately, it takes some time and knowledge for the procrastinator to understand why it is so hard to focus on something and get the things done in the specified time.

Well, the most straightforward answer is you already know that you must do it, but you are not ready to do it. And the reason is you don't yet understand the value of time. It has become a habit to wait until the last minute to get things done. Also, if luck is on your side, you can get the work done even at the last minute.

Regarding the people I mentioned in the introduction, they tend to get things done at the last minute. It makes them feel confident. Thus, they make it a habit to delay work and get it done in the last moment. So, what are the consequences of this behavior? Quality is one. The quality of the work might be jeopardized. But some people don't allow the quality to be affected, such people face other consequences.

For example, let's consider that you have taken a project that has to be completed in two days. But you just wasted a day, so you are only left with one more day. Within that day, you would have to complete the whole project. So, in such a situation you'd have to delay all other scheduled tasks. Going out with your family or friends might get canceled or delayed. Even though canceling plans with friends and family might not affect your project, it will definitely affect your mood.

So you see, the consequences of not adhering to the deadline impacts not only the quality of the work but also your life. You will not be able to manage your day-to-day activities if you don't work on time.

Procrastination is considered unhealthy, and it is impossible to be treated as something healthy. Even if you are a pro at getting things done at the last moment, you will still have to face the consequences. Many people assume that procrastination is okay because they somehow get the work done without compromising the quality. Well, that's not the case. Even if you are getting the job done, there are a lot of problems that you have to deal with when you delay action. Hence, procrastination shouldn't be categorized as something healthy.

That said, now let's talk about the next group of people. They are the ones who deal with anxiety and panic due to procrastination. Even though you know that you are procrastinating, you can't seem to stop yourself from doing it. That's because you have not felt the problem yet. Maybe you haven't lost a huge project due to procrastination yet.

Actually, many procrastinators I meet tend to say they procrastinate because they are lazy, disorganized, or don't even care that they are delaying. They know what's stopping them from being productive, but still, they don't fix the thing that stops them.

Does that make sense? If you know the activity that stops you from reaching your goal, logically you must stop doing that activity. Instead, you keep doing it, and in the end, you lose out.

However, most procrastinators are wise, and they are hard-working individuals. They are capable of doing their work, but they don't do their work on time. And not doing work on time is a huge problem.

Okay, now you are wondering whether you fall into the first category or second, am I right? Regardless of the type, you have to worry about the reasons why you are procrastinating. What if I provide a few questions and you just try answering them? Once you have found the answers, you will be able to find the reason. Or maybe you'll get a clear understanding of your behavior. Let's go:

## Q1. Once you get a project, do you start thinking negatively about it?

Negative thinking is one of the reasons that cause you to delay the project that you must do. When negativity invades, you start questioning your abilities and skills.

You think that you have too much to do and there's so much to research, you believe that you should start it when you are in a good mood. Sometimes, that good mood never comes and eventually, you end up delaying the project till the last minute.

Whenever you get a project, you must believe that you are capable of doing it. You must consider every new project as a challenge. You also need to love the work you do. If you like it, procrastination can be controlled.

## Q2. If you fail, what impact will it have on your reputation?

As I said, some people procrastinate and yet manage to get things done at the last minute. But sometimes, they might also face failures due to their habit of delaying. Just imagine, your habit of procrastination might not have affected your work life yet.

But if it has? What if you get fired due to delaying the projects? How will it affect your reputation? Have you ever thought about this? Most people don't think it through. It is easy for them to keep delaying their work without even feeling the importance of it.

The moment you start understanding the importance of the work and how it might affect your reputation, you'll become organized. Or if you don't, you'll have to face the consequences. I'll be talking a lot about this in the following chapters, so don't worry if you don't find the reason for procrastination in this chapter.

## Q3. If you perform well you might have more

**responsibilities, is that why you don't want to do the work on time?**

You already know that meeting deadlines is one of the essential qualities of a worker. If you do the work on time, you will feel satisfied and great about yourself. There is no need to stress on completing the project.

Almost all negative emotions can be avoided if you stay on track. So you see, working on time has very little to do about others and a lot to do about you. If you think that you'll receive more responsibilities, you should talk to the relevant person and turn it down politely. Only take on what you know you can handle. If you have to take on more responsibilities, look at how they will be beneficial for you!

## Q4. The task should be perfectly done. Do you believe in perfection?

Well, it is good to think about doing something perfectly. But the moment you target perfection, you tend to incur delays. For example, your first draft will not be perfect, but through editing, you will make it perfect. Somehow, we have to spend a little more time to get the final product to the right standard. You must understand that the concept of delaying shouldn't be related to perfection. But most people delay for this reason, they want to get the perfect result, so until they get it, things are held up!

## Q5. Once the task is assigned, do you wait for the right time to start?

Most of the time, the right time never comes until the deadline is close. If you follow the habit of waiting until the right time, you might never get things done on time. I have associated with people, who believe that they should wait for the right time.

Let me mention an example, assume that a project was assigned in the evening, the procrastinator starts it the next morning. If you ask why he/she will say that the project was assigned only after half of the day was gone. Of course, yes, but he/she still had time to, at least, plan the work. The procrastinator who waits for the right time, will not do it. Instead, he/she will waste time and worry later.

**Q6. Once you get a project, do you divide the work according to the level of importance?**

Most procrastinators are good planners, but not good followers. They might plan the project, and they might even divide the tasks as per the level of importance. But they will not follow the way they planned. Instead, they will focus more on less important things and struggle to complete the project at the last minute. Basically, they will not follow the plan they write.

**Q7. If you have two or three weeks to complete a project, do you use the phrase "I'll start tomorrow?"**

If yes, no doubt, you are going to end up impacting your work-life balance. If you neglect the importance of the deadline, you will not be able to get the work done on time. If you don't get things done on time, you will not be able to maintain the balance in your life.

What happens when you don't have the work-life balance? You struggle to hang on to your job while trying to keep the family bonds stronger. Do you really want to have a hectic and an unsteady life and mind?

## Q8. If you have a tight deadline, will you consider doing unimportant things?

If your procrastination level is exceptionally high, you might not consider deadlines as a big deal. You might even ignore them. Or you may even focus on other unimportant things. Some people do such things even if they have very tight deadlines. But remember, procrastination will not let you do anything peacefully.

These are some of the questions that you must ask yourself. I have mentioned certain factors as well. If you have these problems, you can use these questions and ideas to get a clear understanding of the decisions you have and how you should make them.

It might be that procrastination hasn't caused any problems for you yet, and therefore you don't consider it a headache. But if you rewind and see how you reacted and felt when you had tight deadlines, you might sense the negativity it caused. When you delay something, you fear every minute whether the client will ask for the project, every call will create tension, every message, and so on. Do you really want to have to cope with this tension?

Think of procrastination as a cycle of shame, avoidance, fear, and anxiety. If you don't get the work done on time, it will play on your mind until you complete it. Maybe you'll watch a TV series, or perhaps you'll play video games instead of doing the project assigned, but the thoughts will be about messages from your client asking for the completed project. You will not even enjoy the game or the TV series because your mind is tense and it is not at all soothing.

If you had allocated the days and completed the project before the deadline, you could have spent time enjoying your hobbies without any guilt or tension. Think about it, wouldn't it be wonderful? Once you try this, you will appreciate the beauty of working on time.

However, most procrastinators forget the consequences they often face and then, they keep repeating the same thing over and over. I'm going to share a few exercises and tips that you must follow to overcome procrastination.

**Self-Sabotage and Procrastination**

Procrastination has a direct connection with self-sabotage, and there's no doubt about it. Whenever you are procrastinating, you are self-sabotaging. Have you ever felt that way? Usually, people are aware of the things they do, and they know, by doing it they will be rewarded. Yet, they resist doing the things that must be done. It's just like doing wrong to yourself. You become your own worst enemy, nobody else.

As an individual, you will have goals to achieve. You might be working towards achieving them, but then, you get distracted by irrelevant things.

Whenever you get distracted, the unimportant things may look substantial, and the essential elements may look unimportant. If you are dealing with this, it is not because you are unable to perform the task. It is because you are losing the motivation to achieve your goals. This is where self-sabotage comes into the picture.

Sometimes, when you want to start something great, there's something that stops you from doing it. Or sometimes, you might be so confident of finishing a specific project within the given time, but then, you see yourself running behind the deadlines. Why does it happen?

Have you ever wondered about the reasons why such things happen? You have to focus on the underlying reason so that you can take necessary actions to overcome them. However, you must also understand that self-sabotage is related to your mindset. The way you look and see things have a lot of connection to the concept of self-sabotage. Constant failures mean you are not motivated, and it is high time to treat yourself. To make yourself understand the importance of your goals and aims.

Only you can stop self-sabotage because you are the one

who's causing it! How will you do it? You just have to understand and find the pattern, once you do you will be able to work against it! There are two main contributing factors when dealing with self-sabotage: negative thinking and perfectionism.

You must understand that negative thinking is dangerous because it can cause a lot of damage to your productivity. If you are regularly criticizing yourself, you will not be able to achieve your goals or tasks. Maintaining a good relationship with yourself is crucial. You are important. Most people fail to understand their self-worth, and it triggers negative thinking. If you are kind to yourself, you will be able to build a successful mindset, in turn, helping you do better in whatever task you are completing.

Similarly, the need or compulsion to begin only once you have perfected the skill is another motivator for self-sabotage. You assume that there is perfect timing for everything, but actually, it is not true.

The perfect time is when you start the task or the milestone as soon as possible without postponing. Most of the time, when you wait for the perfect time, you tend to lose track of the deadline, and it makes you get things done at the last minute. This will lead to poor work performance.

You must be sure to overcome the two main factors that deal with self-sabotage. Also, know that there are different tools that you can find online to overcome self-sabotage. It is highly recommended to search for tips and tricks to overcome self-sabotage. Learning has no limit, so keep educating yourself.

Accept that you get distracted, if you do, it will not take time to surpass it. The ones who don't accept the truth tend to struggle a lot to overcome it!

# CHAPTER 2: HOW TO REDUCE PROCRASTINATION EASILY

One of the primary reasons for your procrastination habit could be not setting realistic goals. Most people don't set goals, and they start work once it is assigned. Actually, if you don't set goals, you'll not understand the reason for doing something. Everything will seem absurd because you don't know the reason why you are doing it.

When a person sets a goal, it gives him/her a complete understanding of the task that he/she wants to perform. It is more like planning. I'm going to help you learn how to set goals, but before that let's check the common mistakes that a person makes when goal setting.

Why do you set goals? What's the connection between goals and procrastination?

If you set goals, you can quickly reduce procrastination, and the level of productivity will increase. When a person avoids goals, he/she will wander in life because goals are like directions. Do you know anyone who wants to go through life feeling lost?

Luckily, there are so many methods to keep yourself on track. Many tools are available to help in creating and following goals. Most methods are accessible online, which means they are more convenient. But issues can still occur when you don't understand the mistakes that are being made.

If you don't want to make a mistake while setting your goals, you really should read below. I'll discuss the common mistakes associated with goal setting.

### *Immeasurable and not-specific*

This is the most common mistake related to goal setting. For example, if you are a writer and if you want to complete a 2500-word article in a day, you must set a measurable and specific goal. Say, you'll complete 1500 words in the morning and the rest at night. Thus, there's a specific word count, so you know that it is possible to do so.

But what happens when you don't set a specific, measurable goal? You tend to delay. So consider the same example, if you don't allocate certain hours, you might keep saying "I'll start in a while," and this will lead to considerable setbacks. You'll end up rushing at the last moment.

### *Unrealistic goals*

You know how much you can do within a day, so if you know that, you will know to set the right goal. If you aren't sure of what you can achieve, you set unrealistic goals. For example, you might set a goal to read 50 books in a day. Seriously!? Is that even possible? Perhaps if you are gifted with a kind of superpower! When you set unrealistic goals, your mind tends to freeze when they are identified. Once again, you end up delaying the work.

### Not prioritizing

There will be many goals, but you have to learn how to prioritize the important ones. It is pretty easy to set many goals at once, but understanding the goal that requires more time is not easy. You must have the ability to analyze the goals and decide the goal that requires more time and attention first. Then, based on that, you can set your goals. Many people have problems with prioritizing. If you don't have any deadlines, you must focus on the work that might have a significant impact on you, and you can arrange the goals appropriately.

### Not knowing the method

No matter how many goals you have, it is essential to create a plan. Without a proper plan, you will not be able to do the right thing at the right time. In fact, your mind becomes almost paralyzed when you don't have a plan. You might have a lot to do, so without a structure, it becomes severe. If your mind doesn't get the right signals, it will not perform in the way you want. And you will end up delaying the work instead of getting it done. Try to break your goals into smaller sections, so that you are able to achieve them.

## *Not considering the performance*

Once you set a goal, you must not forget that you set a goal in the first place. Many people set goals and forget that they even did it. Even if you don't check your performance frequently, it is essential to check it occasionally. If you evaluate your performances, you'll be able to decide whether you've been working towards your goal or not. That can be a motivation as well.

When you don't measure the performance, it's apparent that you'll delay your goals. Ask yourself whether you've achieved anything from the time you set the goal. Check whether you've gotten closer to your goals than you were before.

These are significant problems associated with goal setting. If you focus on the issues first, you will be able to set the right goals. However, there are specific ways to set goals. So, let's check them out:

## Setting the Right Goals

Often you hear the question "where do you see yourself in five years from now?" but almost all the time, you are unable to answer. Interviewers regularly ask this question, but people rarely have the right answer. If it seems like you don't know the answer to this question, you might not make the impression you want to. It implies you don't have any specific goals. If you don't have specific objectives when you are working, you will not be able to achieve anything. If you think about it, it sounds reasonable.

When you have a specific goal, you'll be able to understand your next step. Start by following this exercise today. What have you decided to do today? If you haven't decided on anything, stop right here. Think about the projects that you have and analyze. Once done, you can set the specific goals you want to achieve today.

For a successful journey, goals are a must! Goals help you stay focused. Once you have goals, you can easily take control of the things that you do. They provide the benchmark to check whether you are accomplishing what you set out to do.

But, how can one set goals without knowing how to do it? You can't just keep saying that you want to achieve certain things. Instead, you must make it happen. Before you set certain goals, you must carefully understand what you really want to achieve. With hard work and determination, it is possible to reach your goals. You must set your steps perfectly, and move forward. So, here are a few steps that you must follow:

### Goals must motivate you

Your goals shouldn't bore you, instead, they should prompt you to move forward. The goals should make you understand their necessity and value. For example, you have been assigned a task, but you are not interested in doing it. If that is the case, will you even try to consider it? More than likely you won't. You will procrastinate as much as you can, and then, in the last moment you'll wrap up the project. This is not going to help you grow because you are completely uninterested in the work. Hence, you must feel and know the importance of a task. You must understand the impact of the task on your ultimate goal. Motivation helps you remain on track.

If you don't have the motivation, you'll not push yourself to do it. Most people tend to set too many goals, and then they get confused. They get confused about which goals they should reach first. They do not know how to prioritize because they have too many goals lined up.

If you want to achieve a goal, it is important to allocate time to understand and commit to it. The urgency to get it done is one of the practices that you need to grasp. When there is no urgency in your goals, you tend to delay them because you think that the goals can wait.

But this reflects on you. You become frustrated about your behavior and you are demotivated. A lack of motivation leads to self-doubt, and you may even think that you can't achieve anything in life.

**Practice 1:** The most important practice that you should know is to write down your goals. The written note will keep you moving forward if you put it somewhere you can see easily and often. You should write down the reasons why these goals are important.

For example, before you write down anything, think about how you'd tell someone the importance of your goal. How will you make them understand that your goals are worth pursuing? So as if explaining it to someone else, write it down and paste it somewhere you can see. This motivation will help you like the bright light in a dark street.

### *Elaborate on the goal*

When your goal is tangible, it has more power and meaning. If your goal is sitting on your table, there's no chance of not seeing it. Even when writing the goal, you must ensure to write positively and with an impact. Add a title like "I will do it today!"

When the goals are positive, they give the vibe that you need. Just try listening to a motivational song or a speech; you tend to feel it in your heart. If you want to carry the motivation throughout your journey, you must write down the goals in the most positive way. The power of your written goal will help you achieve it.

**Practice 2:** The second practice is to write positive goals. You can easily twist and turn words to make something doable; thus, when writing down your goal use the most positive vocabulary. And then, make a To-Do-List to get things done on time. The list should include the goals in the priority order so that you don't have to rush at the last moment.

### *Planning it out*

Not only for work-related things, but also for anything that you want to do in life, planning is integral. When you have a plan, you get to see things straight. You will know what to do and what not to do. Most people don't plan because they think it's extra work. Instead, it is not extra work, it is an outline of the work you NEED to do. If you plan, you will have a systematic way to achieve your goals. When you are organized, you will not move off track.

**Practice 3:** Goal setting means there should be planning. Without planning, goal setting is incomplete. If you want to get a proper outcome of your goals, a plan is much needed. You must write down the steps to achieve your goals. If you normally write 500 words/hr, it will take you 7 hours roughly to complete the project. So you can break the project into 7 smaller pieces. Do it step by step. Once you achieve those steps, you can tick them off. This will help you stay attached to whatever you intend to do. Also, you must keep reviewing your goals so that you can ensure you have achieved them.

### *SMART concept*

You have probably heard of the SMART concept. But do you follow the concept? If you do, you will not have a problem with procrastination because it helps a person to achieve goals easily. If you haven't heard of it, SMART stands for Specific, Measurable, Attainable, Relevant, and Timely.

**Practice 4:** So when you set a goal, you must ensure that your goal goes through the concept of SMART. If the concept of SMART filters your goals, you will be able to have a steady and clear mindset to achieve them. Also, it will be easy to avoid procrastinating.

These are the four main practices that you must follow when you are setting goals. If you follow these, you don't have to worry about delaying your work or being underproductive. Instead of saying that you want your goals to come true, you can actually fulfill them.

Until you get a clear idea of what you are going to do, the rate of success will be lower. Just try setting a goal today, and you will feel that you are more confident and satisfied than the times when you didn't set goals!

"One way to keep momentum going is to have constantly greater goals."– Michael Korda[1]

# CHAPTER 3: BEST ANTI-PROCRASTINATION EQUIPMENT

Like I said, social media has become the most common distraction that people have to deal with. We all know that technology plays a huge part in peoples' lives.

We believe it is also a reason for the problem of procrastination. But ironically, it has the answers to your procrastination habits. Since there is technology, you don't have to worry about ending your habit of procrastination. Why? There are numerous ways to overcome the habit of procrastination.

For example, through motivation, you can overcome procrastination, but apps and tools sound more practical than motivation. So, if you are looking for the best anti-procrastination equipment, know that there are many.

**Small Habits, Big Change**

You already know small habits have a bigger impact on your life. For example, if you brush your teeth twice a day, you will not see the changes right away, but you will have a great set of teeth when you grow old. Just like that, when you practice simple habits now, they will have a massive impact on your life later. So, here are some of the tips that you should follow:

### *An organized individual*

Do you think plans can't change your level of productivity? Well, try creating a plan, maybe for the work you have for next week or the work you have to complete tomorrow. And then, stick to the plan and see what happens.

It might sound simple. You might even wonder if a simple plan can bring so much difference. Well, yes, it can! Through a plan, you organize the work that you have to do. When you organize the work, you understand the process clearly.

For example, you have to complete a massive project, but if you just let the huge project be as massive as it is, you will not feel like doing it. You will not be able to see the amount of work you have to do in a day and that will create boredom and ignorance. That being said, you have to organize the work that you have. Luckily, there are so many great tools and apps that you can find to organize work (more on this later).

### *Make it simple*

Another common reason for procrastination is due to having complex tasks. Of course, some tasks can be complicated, but it is not as if you can't simplify them. For that, you have to set simple, achievable goals. Instead of saying "I'll complete the project" say, "I'll complete the first part of the project today." When you make it sound simple, it will actually be simple.

### Have a schedule

Once you have a goal, it is important to schedule it because scheduled work has a higher rate of achievement. Break your work into chunks and set a deadline. If you set your deadlines, you will be able to achieve them before the actual deadline boggles your mind. Sometimes, you might come across unexpected situations in life, so, completing the work before the deadline will help you stay in the safe zone.

### Set aside distractions

You might already know the things that distract you. For example, if you are addicted to Snapchat, don't keep your phone near you until you get the work done. Or if you are a LinkedIn enthusiast like me, stay offline until you complete the work. Don't even add the Google chrome extension of LinkedIn because it is incredibly distracting. The moment you see the notification, you might want to check the messages even if you have so much to do. It is better to put all your distractions aside and focus on the work you have.

### The Pomodoro Technique

This approach promotes working for 25 minutes and taking a break for 5 minutes. Most people consider this as an effective and excellent solution for procrastination. Honestly, this is a fantastic technique, and you will be able to get a lot of things done if you follow this approach. Moreover, by following this technique, you can ensure the quality of your work remains high as well.

During the break, you must not get distracted, thus do something like listening to music, walking, or even screaming to release stress. Whatever it may be, make sure it makes you feel relaxed and comfortable. The activity that you choose to do should be something that you like, but not so much that it will divert your focus!

### *Reward yourself*

Everybody loves rewards, so it is highly recommended to reward yourself when you follow your plan. For example, if you set a goal to write 2500 words within 5 hours, you must treat yourself once you have achieved it! You can reward yourself with ice cream or an episode of your favorite show. However, make sure that you get back to your routine once you've enjoyed your treat.

### *The myth of doing the hard thing*

So far, you have probably heard that doing the hard things first, helps you get other things done sooner. REALLY? Let me ask that again, REALLY? The rule of doing the hard things first doesn't work for me. If it works for you, then, please ignore this point. But if you give it a thought, you will understand the underlying concept. When you do what's possible, you become motivated to do the hard things too. Besides, when you try to do the hard tasks and they look harder than they first seemed, you might even delay the work. It is usually better to do things that are manageable first.

These are the small habits and changes that you must incorporate to become a productive individual. But there are many more anti-procrastination tips that I want to share with you.

**Getting Started Technique**

If you want to do something, you must get started. People usually procrastinate at the beginning of a project, so it is important to understand the techniques to get started. How can you do it? Starting a project or a task will not be easy; in fact, it can be the reason for delayed submission.

Whenever you plan to do a task, you need something to boost your mood. At first, getting started can be difficult, but when you move on with the task, it might seem possible. Compare the way you feel when you start the work and the way you feel when you delay the work.

Even if you have done a little from the whole project, it's a good start. Starting the project is important, so it doesn't matter if you do even a very little portion of the whole project. There is a trick to make your mind like the work, and that is to start thinking about it.

When you keep your mind occupied with the task, you might somehow end up starting it. The reason is it is tiring to think, so you eventually start work.

For example, say you should edit an article. If you don't begin editing, you will never do it. Start by just taking the draft and change a few words. Eventually, you'll end up changing the major sections that you wanted to change. You will do it even without forcing yourself to do it, which is amazing!

Or you can set a timer. What can you do with a timer if you really can't start the work? Simple, set the timer to 10 minutes or less and then, once the timer starts working you remain seated. Even if you don't do the work, just sit there. Eventually, you'll start work, and you will not even feel that you have started. This is an easy trick because when you are within your workspace, you can't help, but work.

So, these tricks and tips might help you get better at what you are doing. The simplest mantra is "get started!"

**Useful Tools and Apps**

Now that you've learned almost all the possible tips and tricks, it is time to get a grip on the tools and apps available. Beating procrastination will not be easy until you get help from the technology that you blamed for your reluctance. You have so many great tools and apps to select from. We'll discuss a few beneficial tools that you can rely on. Here we go!

## *Procraster*

This is one of the procrastination-busting apps, but compatible only for iPad and iPhone. The app will support you throughout the procedures by providing the right answers and advice for the option you provide.

For example, if you select the option "I don't know how to start" the app will suggest breaking the tasks into chunks. It provides not only ideas but also guidance to do the work. You'll find a rhythm to your work, and you can even check the statistics related to your productivity. The statistics will become a motivation to reach the goals.

## *StandStand*

Anecdotally, it is considered that changes in the working environment can cause positive changes to your productivity. The introduction of the portable standing working table has become a great piece of equipment to fight against procrastination. Sometimes, you might get bored by sitting for long hours, in such a case, you can consider the StandStand table.

The StandStand table helps to increase productivity by allowing you to alternate between sitting and standing at your workstation. Once you change your posture, you'll be able to do focus and get a lot of things done. This is available for purchase on Amazon.

## *Focuswriter*

If you want to type something on the laptop or computer screen, you must make sure that you don't get distracted. It is easy to get distracted when you have the option to open as many tabs as you want. While working on a screen, if you have too many tabs open, it will definitely kill your productivity. So, for that Focuswriter is a great tool. This is a program that works exactly like a Word document. It also has built-in timers, better ambiance, daily goals, and many other options.

This program supports Windows, Mac, and Linux systems. By using this tool, you will be able to do your work on time with better productivity. Moreover, the time that you usually waste can be saved.

## *Freedom*

This app provides peace of mind by helping you focus on the important things and avoiding distractions. Once the app does it for you, you will be able to focus on the work you do. People often procrastinate when they slowly shift from an important task to another entertaining activity.

For example, say that you are working on a project, but meanwhile, you are scrolling through Facebook feeds, so do you really think that you can give your best to work? Probably not! When your attention is divided among other unimportant tasks, you will not be able to give the best to your MOST important project. So, the Freedom app will help you by blocking sites such as Twitter, Facebook, and so on. The Freedom app will block almost all the time-consuming sites. It is strongly advisable to give this app a try if you are distracted by social media.

### *Todoist*

This is one of the popular apps that you might have often come across. People usually procrastinate because of not having a proper plan, or not knowing the task to do next. If you have a structured plan, you will be able to understand the task that you must do next. So with the help of the Todoist app, you can get the structure of the plan.

You can use this app to track and sync the tasks to your mobile and other devices. The app is available for Android, Windows Phone, iOS, and the web. Once you download the app to your device, you will be able to get the To-Do-List!

### *Write or Die*

This is an excellent app for the ones who can't overcome procrastination even after changing their behavior. If you are still struggling to focus even after changing your behaviors, you must take extreme measurements.

The app Write or Die will avoid procrastination by sending annoying pictures and sounds. This is called the Kamikaze mode (derived from the term created from Japanese suicide pilots during World War II[1]).

When you delay work, the vowels on your documents will

automatically be deleted. Perhaps, you wouldn't prefer deleting the words you hardly type. This can be one of the best anti-procrastination equipment.

## *Spotify*

This app will help you stay entertained while you are working. Whenever you find it boring to get your work done, you can play some great music on Spotify. This might help you avoid procrastination. Besides, if you play some motivational songs, you'll be driven to do the work.

## *Tomato Timer*

I mentioned the Pomodoro Technique earlier, and this app relates to it. You usually procrastinate when you don't feel like doing a big task. But you still have to get this task done, and for that, you have to divide the big task into smaller tasks. The Tomato Timer app is the idea to help you to get things done by dividing them into chunks. You just have to set a timer, and then, you will be able to get the work done.

Even though there are many more tools and apps that you can consider, these are considered the most important and beneficial ones! Select the most suitable tool or app as per your preferences and make use of it!

# CHAPTER 4: 27 TACTICS TO BEAT YOUR PROCRASTINATION

I don't think there's anyone who has never procrastinated and it's okay to do so. We are humans, we tend to get bored, and we tend to procrastinate.

That kind of procrastination is okay until you become controlled by procrastination. If you let procrastination rule you, then things will turn against you. It will become tough to achieve the goals that you have set. It is important to beat this habit before it becomes a bad habit.

Luckily, you can overcome procrastination through different tactics. You will be able to command your mind to do the important tasks and to avoid the unimportant tasks. For that, you have to master the following 27 tactics. If you settle for action-related tactics, you will be able to see a great change in the way you delay tasks. Let's get started!

# 1. Move around

If you are a freelancer, procrastination can be your worst fear. You might be working for a long time, but suddenly, procrastination comes into the scenario. In such an instance, you can consider moving around rather than remaining in front of your device.

When you change the scenery, your procrastination habit will not be able to have much of an impact. Once you move around, you will be refreshed to work again. If you remain in front of the device, you might kill time by surfing some other details on the internet. So, it is recommended to move around.

## 2. Let motivation in

You can have someone who motivates you or you can consider listening to and watching motivational videos. When you let motivation into your life, you will become more engaged in the things that you are doing.

There are many motivational speakers, so why not consider some of their videos? You'll feel great about yourself, and your goals will make sense when you listen to those videos. You will be encouraged to work even harder without letting procrastination play a role.

## 3. Set reminders

It is beneficial to set reminders because they will prompt you to remember the activity that you should be doing at a given time. Even if you have not been doing the work, this reminder will become a wakeup call. And you get back to the field without being distracted. There are different ways to set reminders. One of the ways to set a reminder is through motivational quotes. When you set the reminder, it will play the motivational quote when the time is up.

## 4. Innovate

Innovating is one of the methods to stay on the right track. You can create anything you want. Through creativity, you will be able to enhance your mood and interest in the current task. Try making it a habit to do something new every day!

## 5. Early risers

The best thing about being an early riser is that you get to enjoy the stillness and quiet nature. In the morning hours, you will be able to focus on the important tasks and get things done more than at night. Most people have a higher rate of productivity during the day than at night. If you have not tried working during the morning hours, I urge you to try it once. If you do, you will understand how much more productive it is when compared to the nighttime.

## 6. Go to bed early

If you don't sleep early, you will not be able to wake up early. Even if you wake up early, you will be groggy throughout the day. How can you work when you feel groggy? So, it is important to go to bed early. Besides, you will be able to get a good rest when you sleep well. If that happens, your body will be able to perform better, and it will be recharged. If you are tired, you will definitely procrastinate. Give enough rest to your body.

## 7. Be accountable

When you are accountable, you will automatically get the urgency to complete the task. If you want to be accountable, you must make another person aware of it. You must be vocal. You can easily do something to make yourself accountable for the work that you have been assigned. Once you take responsibility, you will ensure to do it even if it seems hard. By being accountable, you can avoid procrastination.

## 8. Get rid of the cable

Most people waste time and money on TV. If you want to save both time and money, you should simply cut the cable. And you shouldn't work in front of the TV because it will be distracting and disorganized. If you want to get the work done in the right manner, you must make arrangements for it.

## 9. Clean as soon as you can

If you wait until you complete the work, you would have to clean a huge mess. Instead of doing it, you can spend around 20 minutes per day to clean. Or you can clean as soon as you can.

For example, if you have taken a half an hour break, you can consider cleaning within that time. But cleaning as soon as you can is suitable for those who identify themselves as clean freaks. That said, if you are not a clean freak, you might find it harder. You must clean just your room or home, but also mental and digital clutter. If you pile up the mess, in the end, you will struggle to declutter.

## 10. Don't think, just do it

Most people have excuses and reasons when they want to delay something. You should not make excuses or find reasons, rather just do it! When you think, you will come up with ridiculous reasons for not doing something. Make sure not to overthink much!

## 11. Have a task list

When you don't know the things to do, you will have a tough time understanding the things to be done. So if you maintain a task list, you will be able to find the tasks that should be done within a given deadline. You must be concise and clear when you are making this task list.

## 12. Scheduling time

If you already know that you have huge tasks to be completed, then, take a calendar and mark the dates with the activities to be done on that day. You will be able to beat procrastination with this method as well. Remember, when you are writing down the activities, they should be achievable, don't add an incredible amount of work to be completed in a day. If you do so, you will procrastinate because you know that you can't do it.

## 13. Stop checking emails

The most common method of wasting time is checking emails while working. Normally, it is not recommended to check emails early in the morning because if you have received negative feedback or replies, it might ruin your day. Thus, let your morning hours be productive as much as you can, and then, allocate some time to check your emails.

If checking emails is something related to your work, then, it is okay. Even then, you should attempt not to open emails that aren't important. By opening non-work related activities, you'll be wasting time. Try to stick to the important emails only!

## 14. Avoid social media accounts

When you start to work, shut off all the social media accounts such as Twitter, Facebook, Instagram, Snapchat, etc. If you keep them open, it is obvious that you'll be distracted. You will not be able to focus on the task you are doing. In fact, they support procrastination above anything else.

## 15. Time your work

As I mentioned in the previous chapter, the Pomodoro Technique will help you get your work done in a short time. If you set a time and work, you will be able to do a lot more in a short time. This will help you become productive while defeating procrastination.

## 16. Keep track of your performance

The best way to find how and where you spend time is by tracking your performance. There are many apps that you can consider if you want to evaluate your performance, so why not give them a try? Through these apps, you can find the weaknesses and work on them.

## 17. Make your own playlist

Find some great music to shoo away procrastination. And then, create a playlist by adding all those songs together. When you are working enjoy that playlist you created to beat procrastination. The music should make you focus on the work, instead of creating outside distractions.

## 18. Overcome the fear

If you fear something, you will procrastinate. You need to look for the things that you are afraid of and then find methods to overcome the fear. If you overcome the fear, you will be able to keep your attention on the work.

## 19. Accept that you can't be perfect

Nobody is perfect because nobody can be perfect. If you try to make something perfect, you will end up delaying the work. Instead of waiting for perfection, you can start the work and then, edit it once you are done with the first draft.

If you hang on to perfectionism, you might slowly sabotage your success. Instead of looking for perfectionism, look for real work. Try to keep your work original, because that's what matters.

## 20. Be mindful of your work

If you know what you are doing, it is unlikely you are a procrastinator. If you are mindless, you will be web surfing, comment flaming, and much more. So, be mindful of your work in order to improve productivity as well as focus.

## 21. Take a break

If you are too strict on yourself, you will not be able to avoid procrastination. It is important to take breaks in between and treat yourself. If you dwell on your uncompleted task, you will become even more stressed about it.

Taking time out will help you become productive. There's no point in staring at the undone work. A break will help you refresh your mind.

## 22. Keep goals

Every day you start with a handful of tasks to complete. But do you just start your day and rush into the work that needs to be completed? Will it help? If you have smaller tasks, you don't have to worry because you can normally get everything done even without a specific goal. But if your tasks are large, you must have goals. The goals will help you reach the tasks accordingly.

## 23. Productivity tools and apps

In the previous chapter, we discussed the productivity tools and apps. Basically, they were about the tools to fight procrastination. So, obviously, they will help you to enhance the level of productivity. As there are so many tools, you can pick your favorite tool and use it to increase the level of productivity.

## 24. Keep yourself entertained

Yes, keep yourself entertained if you want to beat procrastination. There are many ways to keep yourself entertained; for example, you can play an instrument, if that will release stress. Staying away from work for some time will help you regain energy and will beat procrastination.

## 25. Limit your work

If you try to complete too many things at once, you will not be able to achieve anything because you will be stressed when you look at the workload. Begin by focusing on the important projects that require more time and attention. And then, get it done. Once you complete the projects that need to be completed first, you can move on to the next. If you work less, you will not be able to be more productive. Hence, it is better to delegate tasks when you can't manage them or even train yourself to say 'no' if you can't handle the tasks. In this manner, you can limit your work!

## 26. Keep some alone time

Keep some alone time for yourself because it matters a lot. When I say alone time, don't think about spending time by entering the digital world. The digital world overwhelms you and makes things worse. You should let go of that world, at least occasionally. Try spending some time meditating, it might be more helpful than you think. Even allocating a short time for meditation will help you regain focus and energy.

## 27. Don't underestimate

Don't ever underestimate yourself because you are more capable than you think. If you think you are lazy, you are not! You are not a loser, and you CAN beat procrastination and become more successful in your work.

The above mentioned 27 tactics must be followed if you want to beat procrastination. That said, you might find some of these tactics are just not 'your thing' and if so, leave them and stick with the ones that suit you the best. Overcoming procrastination will help you become a productive individual, so decide whether you want to be productive or not!

# CHAPTER 5: SIMPLE DAILY PRACTICES TO OVERCOME PROCRASTINATION

When talking about procrastination, everyone might relate to it because there isn't anyone who could deny it. At least, once or twice in your life, procrastination would have played its role.

Whenever you miss your deadlines, the level of anxiety rises above your head and you are forced to complete the project as soon as possible. But deep down, you know it is impossible to complete because there is so much to do. Yet, you try! Procrastination will make your life miserable, so try not to make it a habit.

Some people want to stop procrastinating, but they are unable to because they don't know how to do it. Or sometimes, they might be missing the motivation they need. And it can be frustrating, I know. You must understand the fact that procrastinating factors differ from one individual to another:

A writer will procrastinate on the project he/she was assigned. And then, he/she must work day and night to complete the project.

A student will delay school work and then, complete it at the last moment.

An athlete will delay medications because they are so concerned about the current game.

If you evaluate each example above, you will understand that through procrastination every individual mentioned in the example will be affected. For instance, the athlete will have to deal with a lot of severe issues if he/she doesn't treat the injury right away. Likewise, there will be a lot of emotional drawbacks as well.

I am going to share some of the practical daily practices that you can follow to overcome procrastination. These practices will help you beat procrastination even if you are feeling lazy or unmotivated. Before you begin reading the practices below, you must bear in mind that you can select any of them. This means you are not forced to perform all the habits below. Let's get started!

## 1. Find solutions to potential emergencies

Procrastination is not just simply a bad habit; rather it is a dangerous one. It will have a huge impact on your health. Sometimes, you might even lose the great bonds that you shared with your family members. They might even come to a point where they assume that you no longer care.

There will be situations in life where you have to deal with unexpected priorities such as death, sickness, and much more. Such situations can't wait because you will have to address them immediately. In such an instance, you would have to drop all the scheduled tasks.

Some other times, great family events might turn into dreadful situations, and you can't avoid them and get back to your work. Emergencies don't come with a warning, so you have to put up with the obstacles they create.

How can you avoid emergencies? Are you going to stop everything and address the issue? Or if you have already delayed the work and then, something urgent comes up, how are you planning to handle it? What might happen when you ignore the emergencies?

To handle emergencies, you have to have a clear picture of the type of emergencies that you are dealing with. You can think about the aftereffects of avoiding the emergency. Or think about the people who are related to the emergency, how will they feel if you ignore it? What are the actions that you can take to solve this sudden issue so that you can get back to work? Or can you put off the emergency issue because it is not life-threatening?

Before you dig in further, let me tell you. If you are working so hard that you don't even have time for your family, it means you are losing a lot of good things in life, there is a lack of balance. You are not living your life — this where the concept of smart working comes into the picture. You can easily get busy and forget about the people around you. Or you can easily put off emergencies that you believe are not important, and those emergencies might actually turn into severe situations. Of course, you might be so busy that you don't even have time for important things, but it is all about your priorities.

No project, appointment, or meeting is worth ignoring for the emergencies that might affect the life of a loved one. I'd suggest stopping other things when something urgent comes up because procrastination is not only about work but also about life. If you address emergencies right away, you won't have to deal with the worst cases down the line.

Most of the time, we think procrastination is all about work and how we delay work. But I hope I have pointed out something that you should also consider.

If you organize work-related activities and complete them before the deadline, or if you have completed half the work already, unexpected priorities might not create a huge impact on your work life. What matters is being organized and knowing how to prioritize your life matters.

## 2. Carry out daily reviews

Another excellent way to avoid procrastination is through

daily reviews. If you allocate ten minutes from your day, you can assess how things are going.

When you are doing the review, you will be able to find the priorities of your day. Then, you can analyze the tasks that will have a huge impact on your short-term goals. To make this review session simpler, consider carrying out a Q&A format.

What are the scheduled meetings that you need to attend? Are there any emails that you must reply to today? Are there any documents that need to be edited today? Are there any appointments that will take more time than you allocated? What are the tasks that require more attention?

Likewise, you should do a Q&A to find out the layout of the day. But you don't have to stick to the questions that I have mentioned. Instead, you can prepare your own Q&A and follow it. If you do this daily review, you will be able to understand the layout for the day. When you have your layout, you will be able to stay on the track. You will have proper knowledge of the tasks that need more time or a quick response. Hence, you will not procrastinate because you are aware that it will impact your goals negatively.

If you want to know one of the best concepts that beat procrastination, it is the Pareto Principle. This is all about an 80/20 rule. Try to learn more about this concept before you apply it to your day-to-day activities.

## 3. MIT's or the Most Important Tasks

It's tough to beat procrastination if you begin your day with a to-do-list that bursts with tasks. You must have a simplified to-do-list if you want to get things done on time and correctly.

How can you simplify your to-do-list? It is pretty simple if you focus on MIT's - most important tasks. You have to settle for the tasks that will have a considerable impact on your long-term goals. This is recommended by many experts who focus on productivity.

My tips are to select the top three important tasks that need to be handled by the end of the day. It is better to pick two important tasks that have tight deadlines and another that will impact your long-term career goal. If you keep an eye on MIT's concept, you will be able to curb procrastination. Once you complete the two most important activities, you will be interested in doing the other activities by the end of the day. And that motivation is very much needed if you want to succeed in beating procrastination.

## 4. The Eisenhower Matrix

Who doesn't like productivity? Who isn't glad when things happen the way they were planned. But sometimes, things don't work as you planned. If your life is anything like mine, filled with constant emergencies and changes, you must have the ability to make quick decisions.

If you want to make a quick decision, you need the support from the Eisenhower Matrix. The founder of this concept,

Dwight Davis Eisenhower, was a general in the army. It was the reason why he invented this concept. It's not always possible to work according to the plan when you are in an army. There will be sudden and important changes. In such an instance, the Eisenhower Matrix concept was the guideline.

If Eisenhower utilized this in the army, there is no reason why we can't utilize this in our lives to avoid procrastination! When you are dealing with this concept, you shouldn't forget the four quadrants related to it. By focusing on the four quadrants, you will be able to approach your day-to-day tasks accordingly. Let me mention the four quadrants in detail:

### Quadrant 1: Urgent plus important

These are the tasks that need to be completed first because they are way more important than any other tasks and they directly deal with your career goals. Plus, you must complete the tasks right away because they are urgent. If you complete these tasks, you will be able to avoid negative consequences. Once you get your Q1 tasks completed, you will be able to focus on other tasks. For example, if you have to submit a project by the end of the day, your complete attention should be given to that project because it is both urgent and important.

### Quadrant 2: Important yet not urgent

The tasks under Q2 are important, but they are not urgent.

Even though they might have a huge impact, they are not as time-sensitive as Q1. Compare Q2 to Q1, and then, you will understand the difference clearly. Typically, Q2 tasks will include the ones that have a huge impact on your long-term career or life goals. Yes, you need to allocate more time and attention to these tasks. But you seldom do it because your mind knows that the tasks in Q2 can wait.

Meanwhile, you'll be focused on the tasks in other quadrants. Don't make this mistake because your long-term goals are the reasons why your short-term goals exist. For example, your health is one of the important factors, so if you don't spend enough time on it, you will regret it. Yet, when you get busy, you are unlikely to spend time on Q2 tasks. Especially, you are not obliged to answer to anyone about Q2 tasks.

### Quadrant 3: Urgent yet not important

The tasks under Q3 are urgent, but you don't necessarily have to spend your time on them. You can either automate or delegate tasks to someone who can handle the work. These tasks are not so important, so it is okay to delegate them. These tasks often come from a third party and the tasks under Q3 will not have a direct influence on your career goals. But when you are handling Q3 tasks, you must note down the tasks that you delegate. For example, if you are working on a time-sensitive project and the phone rings, you might get distracted answering it. Or sometimes, it might not even be an important call. For such activities, you can assign someone. Even if it's an urgent call, you can still assign it to a person who can handle it. Through this, you will be able to manage your day!

## Quadrant 4: Not important plus not urgent

The tasks under Q4 include the tasks that need to be avoided. These tasks waste your time unnecessarily. If you don't spend ANY time on Q4 tasks, you will be able to spend more time on the tasks under Q2. By now, you'll know what Q4 tasks consist of. Anyway, they are activities like watching TV, surfing the Internet, playing games, and much more.

So, should you eliminate Q4? Well, no! You shouldn't. If you don't have a balanced lifestyle, you might even struggle to protect your job. The tasks in Q4 will help you whenever you take a 5-minute break or whenever you want to step away from work. These tasks shouldn't even be in your mind when you are trying to be productive.

To apply the Eisenhower Matrix to your life, start by drawing a table on a piece of paper or your journal. Then, divide the table into four columns and seven rows. Divide the rows according to the days and add the quadrants to the columns. When your table is ready, analyze your week. But don't write anything down yet. Before you start the day, think, analyze again and allocate the tasks as per the matrix. If something else comes up, you must take some time to analyze the nature of the task, and then classify it in the right quadrant.

Once you complete all seven days, you can study the table and evaluate your effectiveness and productivity. This will not be amazing when you try it for the first time, but don't give up. Keep trying, and eventually, you will find yourself spending more time on the important and urgent tasks.

If you keep following this technique, you will be able to structure your day-to-day tasks, and it will help your success become better and better!

## 5. Do it quickly

Sometimes you come across tasks that don't need a lot of time, not even five minutes, yet you delay it. For example, cleaning after having dinner, sending an email, or even changing into your PJs (this is laziness). Even though these tasks don't take much time, you don't do them because you consider yourself too busy.

Your way of ignoring quick or minor tasks is by telling yourself you have too much to do. But the problem is whenever you delay minor tasks, it builds up into a pile, and you might have to deal with huge tasks at the end. If you don't act immediately, you will have a lot to do when you take days off. Also, if you complete the minor tasks quickly, you will be able to avoid them from accumulating into bigger tasks. There are two practices that you should consider if you want to get minor tasks done.

The Two-Minute Rule is one of the practices that you must follow. If you think that the task will only take two minutes or less, you can do it instead of putting it off, can't you? So whenever you come across any minor tasks, think whether it will take longer to finish those. If they don't, why not get them done? Also, if you follow this habit throughout, you will feel that you are removing a lot of negativity and you have more time to spend on important tasks. Besides, you'll feel that you are more organized and than you have achieved more than before.

In contradiction, if you find tasks that will need more than five minutes, you must schedule a time to do it.

The second practice is to single-handle all the possible tasks. Let me describe an example, say that you've received an email and even though it requires a reply, you delay answering it. But then, when you check it later, you would have forgotten the details on the email itself and so you have to go through the whole thing again. Instead of making this simple task a huge pain, you can easily get it done.

The concept of single handling helps you complete the tasks. If you can see the end clearly, you must make the necessary actions. For example, you can do the dishes right away instead of putting it off for later. Likewise, there are many short tasks that you have to complete immediately.

If you follow these concepts, you will be able to complete minor tasks quickly and overcome procrastination. In fact, the stress that tags along with procrastination can also be eliminated completely.

These are the simple practices that will help you beat procrastination. You don't have to worry or think badly about yourself just because you are a procrastinator. We all have been procrastinators at some point in our lives. Everyone can beat procrastination if they try! Now, you have many practical tips that you can follow. You can utilize them and see if there are any changes!

You are way more powerful than you think, so ONLY you can decide whether to become a procrastinator or a productive individual!

# CHAPTER 6: HOW TO CURE LAZINESS AND BREAK LAZY HABITS

Laziness, as we all know, is a quality present in mostly everyone. It is the quality of not being willing to do any work or use energy, more like idleness. Some people mistake it as not willing to do a task that is severe or harsh, but laziness doesn't depend on the difficulty of the task that has to be done.

Regardless of whether it is an easy or tough task, if you are lazy, then you would not bother to do it at all. Laziness is a part of all humans. Everybody feels lazy at certain times during the day. Some people think laziness is a personality disorder, but it is not so. Just like all other habits and behaviors, laziness is also a habit you have gotten used to. It is not a sin to feel lazy, but it wouldn't be right to spend the whole day being lazy.

So, how do you overcome this habit of yours? Well, first of

all, let's see what the causes of laziness are?

• Lack of motivation

• Lack of self-confidence

• Procrastination

• Distractions

• Exhaustion

• Poor nutrition

• Irresponsibility

• Too much of work

The leading cause of laziness is lack of motivation. Many of us are not motivated enough to do the work. Motivation is much needed in everybody's life. You cannot move forward without even a slight bit of motivation.

Lack of self-confidence and lack of interest in that particular activity which has to be done are also causes of laziness. Lack of self-confidence or self-worth means not believing in yourself. If you believe in yourself, you will have the confidence and eagerness to complete all your tasks as soon as possible. Otherwise, you will feel tired and lazy soon. Laziness also comes from procrastination.

As you all know, procrastinating is the act of postponing or delaying a task that has to be done. The only reason why you postpone work is that you are lazy. By being lazy you are piling up the amount of work that has to be done, and you might end up not avoiding the task. So, always keep in mind not to postpone work due to laziness.

Distraction is one of the main causes of laziness. There are many ways you could be distracted. The most common causes of distraction are electronic devices, social media, talkative people around you and thinking about exciting/up-coming events.

Exhaustion or tiredness is another cause of laziness. Having yourself caught up in too much of work and reaching home late, feeling tired and exhausted may leave you lazy throughout the rest of the day.

Poor nutrition is also another cause of laziness. If you do not consume a well-balanced diet, your body would not have enough strength to perform all the needed tasks. Do not mistake a well-balanced diet to include fizzy drinks, fried chips, or junk food. A balanced diet contains more fresh vegetables, fruits and other food with a high nutritional value. Not consuming the right food needed for your body will lead to body fatigue, which ends up as laziness and other severe issues.

Being irresponsible is another a cause of laziness. Most of the time, irresponsible people tend to be lazy. If you are irre-sponsible, you will not bother about work and stay idle. Having too much work can also be a cause for laziness. When you have too much work, you tend to slow down over time, which ends up making you feel sleepy and lazy to continue. Here your brain gets tired and confused as you are overloaded with work. Now you might understand the causes of the lazy habit you have gotten yourself used to.

How do you find out whether you are feeling lazy or that laziness has become a habit in your day-to-day life? Well, ask yourself these few questions.

1. Do you sleep longer than usual?

2. Even after a good night's sleep do you still feel tired?

3. Are you unhappy?

4. Are you worried about something?

5. Do you have too much work to be done?

6. Are you not able to motivate yourself to do your work?

If the answer to these questions is yes, then laziness has become a habit in your life. If you are not happy, worried or fearing something, then you might be depressed as well, and that is what is leading you to be lazy. This is a serious issue that has to be solved as soon as possible.

Normally laziness is a habit that we have gotten used to by our own selves. Therefore, we can get rid of it without much difficulty. But if the lazy habit is due to depression, then it might be a bit tough to get rid of it reasonably. So, it would be wise for you to consult a suitable doctor. But if the cause of your depressed mind is due to personal problems or bad friends, then you could try talking to them and solve the problem or avoid them if you have to. If it doesn't work, then consulting the doctor is the best and safest decision.

Being a bit lazy for a day is not a sin and will not make a huge issue. But if it is something you get used to daily, it can make your day complicated. This can end up in serious issues, stress and tension. Even worse, it could become a habit, which is not desirable. If you understand the reasons why you feel lazy, you will be able to find a way to get rid of that habit. It depends on the reason you feel lazy. Here are some of the ways to deal with laziness.

• Figure out the exact reason for your laziness

• Schedule your daily routine

• Reward yourself from time to time

• Believe in yourself

• Organize yourself and your surroundings

• Have somebody to keep checking on you

• Get advice from successful people

First of all, figure out the exact reason why you are lazy; is it due to lack of motivation, lack of self-confidence, distractions, poor nutrition, workload or any other cause. If you figure out the reason, it will be straightforward for you to overcome this habit. Without knowing the purpose of this habit of yours, it will be a tough task trying to overcome it.

There is a reason behind your laziness. So, find out what it is and work on how to eliminate it from your life. Scheduling your daily plan can also help to overcome your laziness.

This method may apply to those who feel lazy due to procrastinating or having too much work to do. Jot down your daily plan, including times of the day and set aside timed breaks for meals. This way you will be able to complete your work efficiently without stress or tension. Once you get used to such a daily plan, you will become more organized and responsible. Your fear and anxiety will decrease as well.

Another exciting way to overcome laziness is by rewarding yourself. No one is going to reward you daily, so why not do it yourself? For example, plan an amount of work to be done within a certain period and if you complete it accordingly, reward yourself with one of your favorite drinks or maybe a few minutes of entertainment. This way you will be keen on finishing your task as soon as possible.

Believing in yourself will massively help you to overcome laziness. Believe that you will be able to finish the given task within the period, have confidence and keep on motivating yourself. Before starting your task, make a promise to yourself that you will not be distracted by anyone or anything and that you will complete your work within the period. This way you will not want to break the promise made and will try your best to complete your task without any distractions or laziness. You will surely be able to succeed if you have belief and value yourself and your talents.

Another way to deal with laziness is to organize yourself and your surroundings. Disorganized surroundings can make you feel lazy. Keep your home and surroundings clean, neat and well-organized. This will encourage you to keep yourself busy and not just idle around.

A neat and well-organized area will keep your mind relaxed and free of unwanted thoughts and laziness. Also, not only do your surroundings have to be clean and neat, but you too have to be. An unpleasant and dirty space will only mess up your mind and leave you confused and stressed, which will lead you to feel lazy and not bother to do any of your pending work.

Having somebody to keep checking on you is another right way to keep yourself on track. You could choose a few friends or family members who would be keen on dropping you a message or giving you a call to check whether you are doing your work. Make sure the few people you choose are ones who can motivate and encourage you to complete your task no matter what.

The last thing you could try is to get some advice or learn from successful people. These kinds of people will be able to encourage and motivate you to concentrate on your work with interest and get rid of the bad habits, laziness, and procrastination. Apart from these above mentioned long-term steps, you could try a few simple steps to keep yourself on track. Follow these simple tips which could help you feel energetic and think positively.

• Do not do your task continuously. Take regular breaks and go on smoothly.

• Allocate times for your meals. You would not want to skip meals, which could result in health problems.

• Have a plan or timetable for the day. Even if you are not able to complete it all as stated, try to stick to the plan as much as possible.

• Engage in some physical activities, sports or exercises. This way your mind will be relaxed, you will feel more energetic, and you will be able to concentrate on your work much better.

• Try doing something you like during your break times or leisure times. You might have hobbies such as reading, gardening, watching TV and so on. So, why don't you spend your leisure time engaging in one of these?

• Keep on reminding yourself of the benefits of completing all your work on time. You will for sure have hardships and difficulties in your work, but remind yourself of the benefits and advantages of completing your task, This will keep you focused on your work regardless of distractions you may face.

• Get enough sleep. A few hours of sleep is not enough and will leave you feeling tired and weary the whole day. At least 6 hours of sleep is required for our body to be healthy and stable throughout the day. Usually, it is hard to work until late at night. If so, you could go to sleep early and set the alarm to wake up earlier in the morning to do your work.

• Remind yourself of the consequences. You are sure to face troubles if you do not complete your task correctly and within the needed period. So keep on reminding yourself of the consequences, and that will encourage you to do your work as soon as possible.

• Do not skip breakfast. Make sure you have breakfast on time. The food you take in at breakfast is what keeps you going the whole day. If you do not have breakfast, you will not be able to concentrate on your work, and you will feel tired and exhausted quickly.

• Do one thing at a time. If you have loads of work to complete, do them one by one. Do not try to complete everything all at once, as that will end up jumbling everything and you too will be confused. It is better to complete each task one after the other. Order the tasks accordingly and complete them one by one.

• Avoid procrastination. Procrastination is one of the main reasons for finding it challenging to complete your task. Do not get used to this habit, which will leave you being lazy daily. Never delay your work, do it as quick as possible and then enjoy yourself afterward. It is always better to enjoy yourself after completing your work because you will not be able to reap the rewards as much if your head is still overloaded.

• Try to avoid using electronic devices a little while before going to bed. If you go to sleep right after using your phone or laptop, your mind will not be relaxed, and it will be full of those thoughts. Let yourself, and your mind relax.

Getting rid of laziness is not an easy task. But if you give yourself a push, then there is nothing impossible which you cannot achieve!

# CHAPTER 7: HOW TO DEAL WITH PERFECTIONISM

As you all know perfect means something completely free of defects and faults. It is similar to ideal and flawless. The word perfectionism is derived from perfect. It is the attitude of a person who strives to be perfect. If you expect everything to be the best without any faults, then you are a perfectionist. Perfectionism can be related to doing all your work without any fault within limits provided. You may think that perfectionism is a positive quality or attribute, but it is not always so.

Setting high and demanding goals of achievement for oneself can be both a positive and negative experience. Yes, goals and aims are important and essential in life to allow us to work towards a high target, but what if the goals are impossible to reach and you need to make a lot of sacrifices?

That doesn't sound too good, right? Perfectionism can be harmful and may lead to depression and other mental health issues. So how do you figure out whether you are a perfectionist? Here are some signs that may show you are.

1. Never allow yourself to make mistakes

2. Avoid taking tasks which you think you might not be able to complete

3. Focus only on results

4. Fear of failure

5. Avoid procrastination

6. You are not ready to accept defeat

7. You do not like people pointing out your faults

8. You never ask for help from others

9. Get mad at yourself for not doing your best

10. Even minor failures seem huge to you

If you have the qualities mentioned above within you, then you may be a perfectionist. Perfectionism isn't a good attribute. Not only does it affect your mental health but it also affects you physically too.

How can perfectionism affect you physically? When you are a perfectionist, you will try to complete all your work as quickly and as perfectly as possible. That is your only target, and to reach that target you will sacrifice anything you have to.

So, during such times you might skip meals. If you skip meals regularly, it could affect your body and health conditions. You could become weak, and your body would become fatigued. If this continues, it might lead to further physical problems. Many people around the world suffer from perfectionism. It is something ubiquitous. Anything less than perfect is not accepted by perfectionists. The attitude of perfectionists is entirely different and cannot be understood by most individuals.

Well, do you think perfectionists will procrastinate, that is postpone or delay their work? They would never, would they? This is how you can relate perfectionism to procrastination. Perfectionists never procrastinate. The word procrastination cannot be found in the vocabulary of perfectionists.

That's why they are called perfectionists. Perfectionists make a lot of sacrifices. They sacrifice their leisure time, meals, sleep, etc.. If you are a perfectionist, you will understand this.

As we all know, it is more common that people are lazy and procrastinate a lot. That is the difference between average people and perfectionists. Average people too try to complete their tasks quickly and as best as possible. But, they do not sacrifice their sleep, meals and leisure time. They take breaks and engage in other activities when they feel tired or lazy. If you are a perfectionist, you would never do so. Despite your sleepiness, laziness, and exhaustion, you would keep on working to complete your task as perfectly as possible.

Well, if you are a perfectionist, how can you overcome this disorder? Here are some simple tips that you could try. It will not solve your problems at once, but it wouldn't do any harm to give it a try. So have a look at the below-mentioned tips.

• Take breaks while working. If you feel tired or sleepy, leave your work for later and take a rest.

• Do not skip meals. You might be having a lot of work to complete and not enough time to do it all. But, never skip your meals just to complete your work. You could feel dizzy, and your productivity would decrease.

• Procrastinate. It is perfectly fine to procrastinate a little. Do not make it a regular habit, but once in a while would not do any harm.

• Engage in physical activities. Try to engage in some kind of sport or exercise at least once a day. This will keep your body healthy and free of health issues.

• Enjoy a well-balanced diet. Do not get used to eating junk food and fizzy drinks. Eat food that has a high nutritional value including fresh vegetables and fruits. This way your body will stay strong and healthy, preventing further issues, and you will have the energy needed to complete your tasks.

• Be social. Do not only concentrate on your work. Spend time with your friends and family. Talk to them, laugh with them, share your happiness and sorrows and enjoy yourself. This way you and your mind will feel relaxed and free of tension and stress.

• Listen to music. To make your mind relaxed you could listen to some good music. For sure you will feel a lot better, and all your tension will fly away.

• Enjoy your leisure time. Take some time to enjoy leisure activities. You could go out for a walk or simply enjoy reading your favorite book or playing a game.

• Sleep. Do not sacrifice your sleep whatsoever. Typically humans need 6 to 8 hours of sleep daily. If your body does not get enough sleep, it could end up with other health issues and disorders. Your body will start to feel weak, and you will not be able to concentrate on your work properly. Moreover, productivity will be reduced.

These are some simple tips you could try daily. You do not have to try it all at once. But you could start one by one. It will probably be very difficult or even impossible to change your habits overnight. So start with one tip each day, and gradually you will notice the changes within you. By following these simple tips, you could take yourself a few steps away from perfectionism.

Along with these simple tips, there are more long-term practices that you could try, to overcome perfectionism. They are not easy and obviously cannot be developed within a few days, but you should give them a try if you want to completely stay away from the perfectionist attribute you have within you. Have a look at the following ways to deal with perfectionism.

• Recognize whether you are a perfectionist

• Do not look at mistakes as failures

• Set realistic goals

• Do not try to define yourself by your achievements alone

• Lower your standards

• Instead of focusing on the final result, enjoy the process

• Try new methods

• Do not try to please everyone

• Do not be ashamed of yourself

• Do not compare yourself with others

• Give importance to your needs

First and foremost, you must realize whether you are a perfectionist or not.

How will you be able to deal with it without being able to recognize it? Go through the qualities mentioned above and check whether you possess those. If you do, then you are a perfectionist and need to be healed as soon as possible.

Another thing you must do is stop seeing mistakes as failures. Mistakes you make are not failures. Mistakes are a part of everyone's life. And they are perfectly normal. There is nothing to worry about when you make a mistake. Try to view your mistakes as lessons and learn from them. No person doesn't make mistakes! So do not worry and stress yourself.

Setting realistic goals is another way to overcome this habit of yours. Perfectionists set goals that are practically impossible to reach. And once they are not able to complete their task perfectly, they spend time feeling angry and frustrated with themselves. So ensure that you make goals that you will be able to reach. This way you will be able to take breaks and enjoy yourself too.

Another important strategy is to not define yourself by your achievements alone. This is an attribute of perfectionists. They define themselves by the goals they have reached. Learn to define yourself by your character and personality. Achievements matter too, but character and personality are more important. Perfectionists do not understand this, and that is why they strive to do their work perfectly without faults.

Perfectionists always want everything to be the best. They set standards that are too high. Instead, try slowly lowering your expectations of what a finished product entails. This way you can gradually step away from the perfectionist quality that has grown within you. A critical aspect of all perfectionists is that they focus only on the final result. If you do so, you will not enjoy the process, and you will only try to complete your task as best as possible. This would not be interesting at all. To make your work interesting, enjoy the process so that you'll end up with amazing results.

Another approach you can try is to attempt new methods. Do not keep on doing your work the same way you have been doing for days. Try new methods and ways to complete your work. Usually, perfectionists do not try new methods as they are afraid of making mistakes.

But as stated earlier, making mistakes is normal and there is nothing in it to worry about. Perfectionists need to step outside their comfort zone, so try new methods, make mistakes and learn from them.

Also, do not try to please everyone through your achievements and perfection. Believe me, no one else will bother. By doing this, you are only putting pressure on your own self. Learn to be true to yourself. Try doing things for the experience because you've wanted to try them. It's not always about winning, some things are worth doing, even if the outcome is imperfect.

Being ashamed of yourself is another quality of all perfectionists. Never be ashamed of yourself or your mistakes. Nobody is perfect, even though you think you may be. Everybody makes mistakes and is imperfect. Learn to love your imperfect self. So never be ashamed of yourself, you are beautiful with your imperfections. One of the most important steps to overcoming perfectionism is to stop comparing yourself with others, their work, and achievements.

We grow up in a competitive world, and we develop the feeling of 'not being as good as another' within us. This is very harmful and can result in stress and depression, which will then lead to severe issues. Comparing ourselves with others will only reduce our self-confidence and increase our fears and worries. This is not something anyone would want. So, try your best not to compare yourself with others and their achievements. Everybody is different and has different talents and goals. Focus only on yourself.

And one more strategy to help you deal with perfectionism is to put your needs in front of you rather than putting them last. Know that denying your needs can have serious health consequences both physically and mentally. Never ignore your needs due to your work pressure. Take some time for the things you need and desire. This way your life will be happy and free of stress and tension.

I hope these steps will help you overcome perfectionism. Dealing with perfectionism is not something that can be achieved overnight. It will take a long time, maybe months.

But never lose hope, you will be able to overcome this attribute of yours. Know that by trying to get rid of perfectionism, you are choosing to accept yourself the way you are and enjoy your life with the imperfections, without feeling ashamed of yourself. You are choosing to let go of comparisons and the need to prove yourself. This can be accomplished gradually by loving yourself unconditionally, making some time for your own self, putting your needs first and finally and most importantly reminding yourself that perfection isn't your goal.

# CHAPTER 8: HOW TO USE GAMIFICATION TO STOP PROCRASTINATING

Procrastination is taken lightly by many, but this topic won't be discussed to a great extent. Procrastination can be a hindrance to your career. You may delay work today, and it will bulk up for the next day, resulting in a waste of time and energy. Though you try hard to overcome procrastination, it is a hard task.

There are different solutions to overcome procrastination. One method is to motivate yourself. Such motivation can lead to an increase in your ability to engage in work. But motivations differ. Sometimes, the things I get motivated by may not be the same things that you get motivated by. So it all depends on the individual.

As humans in society, we all need some kind of motivation. You may have a goal to achieve, but if you are not motivated enough, you might lose focus. Some people will have great motivation at the beginning of work, but gradually it may decrease which will also impact your willpower, and automatically procrastination comes into the picture.

To end procrastination, you should not stop motivating yourself. You should also punish yourself if you fail to be organized. By punishing yourself, you can reduce the instances of procrastination. These punishments are not to turn you into a negative person or to make you feel bad about yourself, but to correct yourself which is favorable for you. Let me explain to you some of the ways to motivate or punish yourself.

### Make It Hard To Procrastinate

From the time you wake up, you are distracted by many things, like social media, gossip, and family responsibilities. To beat procrastination you should make it difficult for yourself, but how can you do that? For example, if you are a person addicted to a certain social media app (let it be Facebook, Twitter or Instagram) make a vow to yourself to deactivate these apps until you meet your deadline. As a member of a family, you will have responsibilities that you cannot get rid of, but you can handle your responsibilities if you don't procrastinate. Although you try to fit your goals into the day, there will be various distractions from different directions. Even if things get tough, you shouldn't let procrastination play a role.

### Spend Five Minutes

The Five Minutes concept is about spending five minutes to go through the tasks instead of just thinking about them. Once you go through each one, you'll understand them better. You'll realize the importance of going through the tasks. This is a good method to overcome procrastination.

Let me give you a simple example, if you have a project of around 15 pages, without starting the work you sit and think about the number of pages. Maybe the pages have simple information for you to go through, but you may make it a big issue by just thinking about pages. Instead, you can start the work, which may take 5-10 minutes, but if you start by thinking about the pages, you will waste extra minutes, a classic form of procrastination. By preparing yourself for this method, you will understand that the 5-minutes is more important than the 20 minutes.

### Punish Yourself

This may sound a bit harsh, but for some, though they try different methods to overcome procrastination, they still fail. One reason may be that they still have not understood the depth of procrastination.

To punish yourself you can ask for help from a friend of yours. You can set some strict rules so that your friend can check whether you adhere to the rules or not. It is funny when you think of punishing your own self. Thus, a friend's help can be a great choice. If your friend is concerned about your well-being and productivity, he/she will not pity you while doing the job of an invigilator. When selecting a friend to do this part, you must make sure to consider a lot of factors. This might seem fun and exciting, but this is a serious issue.

## Treat procrastination like a game

Your goals for today are unaccomplished, sitting in a place and remembering that you are a failure is painful, and I accept that. You must find the reasons for not achieving the goals. What could be the reason? Maybe it's a lack of motivation. But here I will give you tips to boost yourself. Turning the daily tasks into games is a way to overcome procrastination.

Introducing games to accomplish tasks is a trick that has a hugely positive effect on the individual. By gaining a victory, you will feel like you have accomplished a huge task. This is because the games encourage you by giving milestones, which triggers dopamine to be produced in the brain, and this dopamine reinforces your desire for compliments and motivation.

There is a correlation between games and procrastination.[1] Gamification is an excellent concept that you should consider if you want to beat procrastination. Now, let's explore some of the most effective ways to gamify your life.

## The Inbox Zero

You already know that your productivity dies the moment you scroll through emails. This is why it is important to consider the Inbox Zero method. What does this mean?

Well, inbox zero means having nothing to do in your email, so that you will not waste time handling emails. For this, there are many apps such as CloudMagic, Boxer Lite, etc. These apps provide options to delay, skip or forward the messages.

### Reward yourself

Preparing a to-do-list using a game will motivate you more. It is straightforward; you will get points to tick off the list when you finish it. If you consider apps like Todoist, you can find ways to gamify the tasks, and it will keep you motivated to complete them.

### Create-your-own system

Implementing gamification into your lifestyle is a common system; this technique can be applied in the following ways. First, is deciding the goals for the day. Next, determine the number of points to be given for accomplishing the goals. The third step is to keep track of the progress toward the goal. Fourth, is to make some modifications such as adding your favorite gaming techniques to motivate and finally reward yourself according to the points acquired. You can use a productivity app like Habitica to make this even more exciting.

These are some ways to incorporate gaming techniques to help you achieve your day-to-day goals. Apart from this, you can also challenge yourself by creating a deadline for a task to be completed. For example, you must finish cooking a special meal before a song ends, or you have to shower before you finish the song. You can set any type of deadlines you like. But the deadline should motivate you to perform the task. By doing these, you can overcome the procrastination to a great extent.

### Promise yourself a reward

Awarding a treat or prize for overcoming procrastination will help you to do better. Rewards can be small or large but should be something you enjoy. The reward will motivate you to stay on task. You can reward yourself with a delicious cup of coffee, or an episode of your favorite series, or your favorite music, or even an adventure. But these rewards should not be another reason for you to turn into a procrastinator. If you have to spend more than 5-10 minutes, better find some other ways to reward yourself. This rewarding method has worked for many individuals. Give it a try, and you too will feel the difference. Remember, rewards are also part of the motivation; don't make them a reason to delay!

### Temptation Bundle

In recent research[2], they have found that instead of rewarding after the goal is achieved, you can reward while following the goal. This will motivate you to put more effort into the process.

For example, you can watch an episode or listen to your favorite music while doing household chores or while at the gym. Students who study for their finals tend to procrastinate a lot. They spend 5-10 minutes to have a cup of coffee rather than utilizing their time better and drinking the coffee while reading a passage. By doing this, they are motivated to accomplish the target.

Obviously, as humans, it is hard to overcome temptations, and for that, you can connect the temptations to your goal. For example, you can have a meal in your favorite restaurant while scheduling the meeting with a client, or you can get a pedicure while scrolling through the emails.

# CHAPTER 9: 10 TIPS AND TRICKS TO GET THINGS DONE IN LESS TIME

Another type of procrastinators are the ones who look for perfectionism. They wait until the last minute to start the project. Even when they are starting the project, they tend to complain about less time to complete it. These procrastinators have a habit of finding great explanations as to why they delay the job.

That's one of the traits of procrastination that we have already discussed. You might be busy, and you have a lot to do, but overworking is not the way to become a productive individual or to avoid procrastinating. When people struggle to meet deadlines, they try to shift the blame to the deadline, but it is crystal clear that the deadline has nothing to do with their delay. It is solely their mistake because they have been procrastinating. Most people rarely accept it.

If you wait until the deadline, you will not be able to work with a relaxed mindset. If you don't have a relaxed mindset, you will not be able to give your level best.

I'm not saying you will become a productive individual right after you read this book because it is not possible. But you must try to bring one change at a time. If you are proactive, you can overcome procrastination.

### Accept the fact that you don't like to work under huge pressure.

Some people actually enjoy working under pressure, such as lawyers, ER surgeons, and politicians (no pun intended). If any of these are your job, that's great! If you think that you are great at working under pressure, you're mistaken. The underlying reason why you are overworking is that you have delayed the work and you must work hard if you want to complete the project. Moreover, you don't want to under-perform, and that's the main reason why you accept that you work well under pressure. The only option you have is to not to wait until the last minute to complete a project.

### Don't avoid the Pomodoro Technique

We have already discussed this method. Through this time management technique, you can manage your work. You will be spending 25 minutes to do the work and 5 minutes to relax. Whenever you have delayed a task or whenever you are assigned a big project, you can follow this technique. Instead of thinking things like, "I'd have to spend my entire life to get this project done," you can say, "I'll follow the

Pomodoro Technique." When you know that you only have to focus on a section for 25 minutes and then you can take a five-minute break, it will help you stay focused. This is one of the best methods to get things done.

### *Do what you can*

For example, you might have to write an eBook. Then, you have to divide the book into a few chapters. If you have divided the chapters, you will feel as if it is manageable. Besides, there might be chapters that are easy and some that are more difficult. However, not everyone can work based on the level of difficulty. So, if you feel like doing the first chapter, just go ahead and start writing. Don't think that you have to do the hard ones first and the easy ones later. It doesn't happen that way. You must do the things that you can!

### *Appoint someone*

You must appoint someone who will follow up with you when you don't meet the deadlines. It can be your parents or friends, but you should be accountable to them. You can ask them to question why you haven't met a certain target that you set. But it is important for that individual to be steady and stern with you!

### *Don't multitask*

You might have been brainwashed to believe that multi-tasking is beneficial. But trust me, it is not! Whenever you multitask, you tend to lose concentration on all the tasks. Of course, some rare people can multitask, but if you are not one of those people, you shouldn't try it. Through multitasking, you will be compromising the quality of all the work, and it will lead to further issues. Besides, it might even make you procrastinate the work. Instead of multitasking, you can do one task at a time and do the best that you can for that particular task.

### Exercise

If you think exercising while you have work to do is another way of procrastinating, it is not true! When you don't get sufficient motivation to do something, it is easy to get distracted. It is easy to avoid doing it. When you are not in a mood to work, you are more inclined to procrastinate. Instead of procrastinating, you can try focusing on some exercise. The exercise will boost your endorphins, and it will make you excited. There are many exercises that you can search online, so find some and save them. Whenever you feel low or underproductive, you can use exercise to boost your mood!

### Know that you are guilty when you procrastinate

Even though we all procrastinate, we tend to feel guilty about it once we face the consequences of it. There can be times when you missed a lot of great rewards just because of your procrastination habits. And there can be days when you worked the whole night to meet the deadline. There can be times when you ditch friends so that you can submit the project before the client gets mad at you. Think about all these situations and accept the fact that you are guilty of being a procrastinator. Once you accept this, you will be able to overcome the issue slowly. Also, acceptance is the best way to get things done.

### Think about the result

What will happen if you delay this task? What could be the worst result of delaying this project? Like I mentioned earlier, procrastination correlates with fear. You can use this fear against procrastination. How? It is pretty simple. You just have to think about the aftereffects of delaying a project. Imagine your boss's angry face or your colleague's frustrated look. Somehow try to picture the consequences of delaying the project. And when you do, you'll automatically fear the mess that you are going to create. And so you will try not to delay the work. The technique of turning fear in your favor will help you avoid procrastination.

### Treat yourself big

Sometimes, small rewards might not satisfy your hunger for appreciation. Also, if you are better than before at avoiding procrastination, it means you must reward yourself big. You must decide to do something that you LOVE once you complete the project. The burning need to enjoy will make your work better, and you'll be more productive.

### Just do it

Like the famous slogan says, "JUST DO IT" because you have to do it! It's your job, and it's your project. You have taken the responsibility to do it, so you can't avoid or find reasons not to! A very common reason for procrastination is not having the urge to complete the task. Why don't you feel like completing the task? The answer doesn't matter because if you have taken up the task, you are responsible for doing it, so, just do it! You must understand the fact that you have taken on the work. Hence you must do it. Let that sink in. If it does, you might find yourself not waiting until the last minute to complete a task.

That said, getting things done is all about how you think! Your mind is the triggering factor to get things done. Think. Perform. And win!

# CHAPTER 10: A FEW THINGS THAT YOU NEED TO KNOW ABOUT PROCRASTINATION

Have you ever heard of people avoiding success? Yes, you have. It is just the term "procrastination" is confusing you. If you are procrastinating, you are avoiding your success, an idea that probably stirs up upsetting emotions. Like we discussed in the previous chapter. You are self-sabotaging! It is not something great because it kills your overall performance. You are creating your own obstacles and hurting yourself.

Why do you do it to yourself? Did you know that some people are procrastinating on purpose? Yes, they are the ones who don't mind delaying the work because it has become a common thing for them. They don't clear bills on time, and they don't clear tax files. Or they don't even do shopping until they run out of groceries. So you see, it has become common and they don't mind being called a procrastinator.

Actually, procrastination is not only about time management and planning. There is more to it, and we'll find out more about it below. We can't say all procrastinators are optimistic, but there are some who think positively. Also, some procrastinators will not even consider your suggestions because they are too positive.

You must also accept the fact that every procrastinator is made, not born. Most people learn procrastination from their families and parents. Even though it doesn't happen directly, the habits eventually get incorporated. One of the most common cases is living with authoritarian parents. They tend to set harsh rules that make the child disobey. They become rebellious. When they become rebellious, they will not listen to what others say or work according to certain rules. Some kids tend to carry this into their adult life as well, and it can restrict their success. In fact, some kids and teenagers who procrastinate tend to rely on their friends more than parents. This will have a negative impact because friends might put up with all their excuses and it is how their habit of procrastination develops.

Procrastinators often lie to themselves. How can you lie to yourself? Simple, putting off urgent work and saying that you can get it done tomorrow is the biggest lie that you tell yourself. And another one is, "I work well under pressure." Well, you do, but then, right after the work is done, you get tired both mentally and physically. And you struggle to give your best for the next work. Likewise, procrastinators are liars, and they don't even mind it.

Normally, they look for distractions on purpose and waste time. The best example is by checking emails. They waste time by doing it and later, they blame the tight deadline because they could not complete the work on time. When you go deeper into the concept of procrastination, you may find a lot of interesting theories and concepts, but I'm not going to discuss those here. You may wish to look into it; knowing a little bit about procrastination is very much important because you will be able to find the rooted factors that lead to procrastination.

Along with the reasons mentioned above, there's another important factor that most people keep forgetting, and that is your health. If you consider the diseases and health problems that accompany procrastination, you will never procrastinate. Some of the common issues are flu, colds, and issues with the immune system, gastrointestinal problems, and even insomnia. Why insomnia? When you delay work you have to be awake the whole night to complete it so eventually, you will feel as if you can get the work done at least by staying up at night. It becomes a reason and a great power, so you make it a habit and procrastinate often. Even though you will not see any health issues right away, over the course of time, you may face a lot of issues. Therefore, it's another good reason to try to stop or at least minimize procrastination as soon as possible.

If you don't overcome procrastination, it will overpower you little by little. Can you imagine slowly losing control? How do you feel when you are emotionally imbalanced? Angry? Frustrated? Obviously, you might get irritated because it is not beneficial to let emotions control you! It makes you vulnerable, so don't allow procrastination and negative emotions to take the wheel.

# CHAPTER 11: THE POWER OF WILLPOWER

Before discussing willpower, let me explain to you the meaning of will, which means the desire or determination to do or to get something. Either you process the work or a second person process the work for you. If you have the will to succeed in the work, you will put in the maximum effort to reach the goal.

The society we live in will provide you with many obstacles and barriers but, if you are a person with strong will then you can break those barriers to reach your destination. When you have an iron will, people may tag you as willful, but you should not stop listening to your desires. Will is connected to desires and passion. Many of you may have a particular passion, but a lack of will may have led you off track to where you may have lost the drive. When you want something, you should also develop your will alternatively so that you push through any challenges.

Now, let me explain to you what willpower is. It is the primary tool to exercise the will you have. You can cross all the obstacles and break all the hindrances in the path to success if you are a person with strong willpower. The majority of the influential people in society are the ones who choose to act on the power of their will. Therefore if you have a strong will and power, your goals can be achieved.

### Willpower vs. procrastination

Now, let's understand the concept of procrastination and willpower. Procrastination can be a reason for you to delay your goals, but this procrastination should not define you. Let me easily explain this to you, you may be a creative person but just because you delay the work doesn't mean that you are a lazy or bored person.

It is apparent that your mind gets triggered in a positive way whenever you listen to motivational videos. Nowadays, you can easily access motivational videos without much effort because of the Internet. You might not accept this concept right away, but try listening to motivational videos, and you will slowly develop your willpower.

It is important to have steady willpower if you want to fight procrastination. When you are invested in a goal or even a project you need to have strong willpower to finish it by the deadline. But how can you do that without procrastinating?

## *The reason behind the goals*

There is a 'why' behind the selected goals, to find the reason for 'why' you should have self-motivation and self-worth. You should be able to find out the reason behind selecting a particular goal. While finding reasons, you should also develop strong willpower.

Now, you know how to find out the reasons for the goals, but you may have a question in your mind, how to overcome procrastination? Before finding out the steps to overcome, you should understand that the reason for your behavior is not that you are lazy or inactive, but you do not want to experience pain or stress in the process. For this reason, you procrastinate. Now the question is how to overcome this. Let me help you!

Fear is a simple word to pronounce, and it is a dangerous weapon that halts people from accomplishing their target. There are different types of fear, for example, some individuals may fear rejection, and some may fear public speaking. Fear stops the motivational function of your brain, but you should not allow this fear to get involved in your thoughts. You should take some time to investigate the things you fear and then find ways to stay focused.

Do regular meditation and exercises that will help you to reduce your stress and fear naturally. At a point, if you realize that you are going back to your old behaviors or patterns terminate the fear in that instance without delaying. After you find out the things that you fear, create a background that will motivate you. The background is a reason for you to become a procrastinator; when you live in a dull environment, your productivity will decrease so make sure to select a better background.

Changing your current lifestyle or routine will also provide a positive outcome. To change this, you can schedule your day by allocating time for exercises and meditation. Also, unhealthy relationships can become a barrier to your goals; if so detach yourself from such relationships. When you have finally started checking off the above points, you can now train your brain to remove the negatives and start thinking positively. And positive thinking is essential to attain your goals. When you distance yourself from negatives, you will find the willpower to exercise your goals.

Now you know what willpower is and the effect it causes on the body and the brain.

### *Try to understand the ways to tackle stress*

Stress is the most used and common word you may hear around, from a kid who has a lot of homework to a man whose deadline for the project is near. Everybody complains about stress. Due to stress, you may make decisions based on momentary outcomes. When you have high-stress levels the energy in your body will slow down. When your energy is slow, the output of the day will be reduced, which will lead to procrastination.

Breathing is a prescribed exercise for stress, so when you are stressed, you can consider this therapy. It is not something that will cost you a lot of money, nor do you need a special time or any equipment. Just breathe. Sit in a quiet place and breathe in and out slowly. While doing it, focus on your breath by paying complete attention to it. I assure you, you'll feel better.

### Stay focused on the plans

While you work or study, you will find varieties of distractions like phones, televisions and various devices. But you should stick to the plan no matter what the situation is.

Let me give you a good example. First, know the difference between "I can't" and "I don't." Can't is what is stopping you from reaching the goals, while don't will hold you to the track and stop your bad habits. Therefore according to studies, it is shown, considering the term don't for your bad habits is better than pushing yourself towards cannot![1] For example, if you say I *don't* want to delay that task instead of saying I *can't* delay that task, you'll spot the difference.

### Get enough sleep so that your brain rests

Getting an adequate amount of sleep is essential for better living; it is found that a person whose sleeping time is less than 6 hours will have a less productive outcome. When your sleep time is reduced, the part of your brain that responds to stress will not work and thus will not help you to detach from stress. You may wonder what the average amount of sleep an individual should have is. A recent study has shown that an adult's ideal sleep time to be 7-8 hours[2]. Perhaps, if you follow this pattern, you can relieve yourself from stress and anxiety.

## *Consider meditation as much as you can*

Meditation or relaxation of the mind is connected to the willpower. It is said that meditating for at least eight weeks (20 minutes each day) helps you to increase the energy, self-management, and awareness. So, my suggestion is to engage in meditation. Through meditation, you can easily tackle your mind and encourage it to work as per your rules.

## *Focus on nutrition and workouts*

Workouts and balanced nutrition will help you to bolster your willpower and your goals. But how can these two factors affect willpower? By developing physical well-being, not only the body but also the mind can be developed.

There are exercises for both body and mind like yoga so that you can train your mind to relax when you are stressed. Excellent plant nutrients found in foods such as grains and seeds will also help you to improve your willpower. If you start looking into nutrition and workouts, keep an eye out for links to willpower. Try to find out more and more information on willpower, and how it may affect your capacity to handle procrastination.

# CHAPTER 12: ONE POWERFUL METHOD TO GET EVERYTHING THAT YOU WANT IN LIFE

## *Know Why the S.M.A.R.T. Concept Is Crucial*

When you are dealing with the concept of procrastination, it is apparent that you will come across the SMART concept too. But why is this? What has the SMART concept got to do with procrastination? Sometimes, we fail to find the connection, and it is the very reason why we fail to achieve our goals. We have spoken a lot about procrastination, so you know what it is. But in this chapter, I'll cover the SMART concept. Once you learn this concept, you will understand the relationship between procrastination and SMART goals.

The SMART concept is used in goal or target setting. Goal or target setting is the process of figuring out our goals and what we have to do to achieve them. Everybody has a goal in life. Setting goals gives our life a direction, and we will be motivated and driven to reach our goal as soon as possible. This is the way we can become successful in life. If you do not have a goal right now, make sure to think wisely and set goals for yourself. The goals of each and everyone of you differ.

You do not have to worry about whether your goal is big or small. The only thing that matters is what you have to do to achieve that goal and whether it is possible for you to do so. Without objectives, life becomes a play that you do not control. Accomplishments such as traveling to space, inventing robots, improving smartphones, and many more, are the results of proper planning and goal setting. Decide your targets and goals based on your skills. You shouldn't underestimate yourself. As an individual, you have the skills and talents to meet any goals. But then again, if you don't move out of the place where you are comfortable, you will not be able to achieve all your dreams. It is highly important to extend your path and your abilities to the areas where you don't feel comfortable.

When you are selecting a certain goal, you must not focus on others' opinions because that is not your concern. Instead, you must focus on your own goal. When you are setting your goal, you must make sure to keep your values high. If you don't respect your value, others will not!

Keep going back to your values and expectations when you

set goals. Once you set goals, make sure you discuss them with experts or people experienced in that particular field. Take their wishes and opinions into account too. Always remember, rather than making a decision all by yourself, it is better to get some ideas and guidance from supportive people. Everybody is different and has different goals and aims that could be in a wide range of areas or fields. Here are some of the different areas in which you can set goals if interested.

• Education

• Career

• Family

• Hobby or Personal interests

• Personal development

Have you heard of the SMART concept in goal setting? In corporate life, SMART goal setting is one of the most effective and yet least used tools for achieving goals. Once you have marked the outlines of your project, it's time to set specific intermediary goals. With the SMART criteria, you can evaluate your objectives. SMART goal setting clarifies the way goals come into existence. If you ask a successful person, he/she will clearly say that goals were the reason for their success. They set goals because it helps them travel to their desired destination. But when you can't easily reach your destination because there are a lot of issues that you have to deal with, the SMART concept can make it happen. SMART stands for:

S – Specific

M – Measurable

A – Achievable

R – Realistic

T – Timely

Let's explore in detail what each letter denotes:

## 1. Specific

When you are going to set a goal, be specific on what you need to achieve. Always be stable and do not hesitate in your decision. Once you have figured out your goal, the next thing you have to do is check what steps have to be taken to reach your goal. Make sure to set a deadline for you to complete the tasks. If you do not have a limited period within which you have to accomplish your aim, you will surely procrastinate. Be specific on how where, when, why and what steps should be taken.

## 2. Measurable

This is about the metrics that you are going to use to identify the goals achieved. Once you focus on metrics, you will see that the goals are tangible. If your goals are measurable, it will be easy to complete them. You can set milestones by focusing on the tasks and the time required to accomplish each one.

## 3. Achievable

Is your goal attainable? That means investigating whether the goal really can be reached by you. You weigh the effort, time and other costs your goal will take against the profits and the other obligations and priorities you have in life. If you want to accomplish a goal, you must have the resources such as money and time, if not you will be disappointed. That doesn't mean that you can't wish for something that seems impossible; you certainly can. But remember, you can only make it happen by planning smartly.

When you identify the goals you want to reach, you begin to figure out ways you can accomplish them as quickly and as productively as possible. You will develop the skills, attitudes, and abilities needed to reach them. Make sure to plan your steps wisely. Through proper planning, you can go a long way. Plus, complicated goals that you believed might take more time will become simpler and achievable. Your goals will have a closer link with yourself.

## 4. Realistic

Goals must represent objectives that you are wholeheartedly ready to achieve. You can set extraordinary goals, but make sure that they are possible. It is important to evaluate your talent as well because if you don't have the required talents, how can you achieve the goals? Your skills are also part of looking at goals realistically. But, remember one thing, usually high goals are more comfortable to reach than a low one because you will not be motivated and energized enough while trying to accomplish small goals as you think it can easily be attained. Meanwhile, you will be well promoted and motivated when working on trying to achieve higher goals.

## 5. Timely

Every goal you set should be given a period within which you have to try and reach it. Otherwise, there will be no urgency in your work. If you do not set a deadline, you will procrastinate, and that would end up with you not succeeding in reaching your goal.

## The SMART Concept and Procrastination

You've probably been wondering about the connection between these concepts, so below you'll find detailed information about the concept, and you will also find ways to utilize it in order to overcome procrastination.

You can now say that you understand the SMART concept and related information. In brief, you can say that the SMART concept gives us steps in how to reach our goals. There can be times when you work so hard, yet achieve nothing. But why does it happen? How much improvement have you seen in your skills and achievements over the past few years? Is it only a little? Then what is the use of so much hard work all these years? Why are you not able to improve your skills?

There are so many questions like this you can ask yourself. And if the answer to the questions is a 'yes,' then know that there is something wrong in the way you work. The problem is in the system of your work, but not in you! The SMART concept is the best solution to make things work for you. As it filters your goals through specific, achievable, realistic, and timely options, you can decide whether or not you are progressing. In fact, the SMART concept will help you identify the reason why you haven't been progressing so far. You must try to reflect on your previous goals and redo them as per the SMART concept. If you do so, you will find yourself achieving the goals before you know it.

So, how can you put forward the SMART concept in the process of creating a goal? It's very important when setting SMART goals to express it positively. Always have a positive mindset, and everything will turn out positively.

The SMART concept can be related to procrastination. As you all know, procrastination is the deliberate delay or postponing of tasks. It is a common habit of most people. Everybody procrastinates, and there are several reasons behind it. It could be because you are sleepy, tired, exhausted or many other reasons. Procrastination is an act loved by most people. It is not harmful to procrastinate once in a while, but make sure not to get used to it on a regular basis.

Regardless, the SMART concept cannot be adequately implemented by people who procrastinate. If you keep on delaying or postponing your work, then what is the use of following the SMART concept?

If you plan to reach your goal according to the SMART concept, you must make sure not to procrastinate too much. But of course, that doesn't mean you cannot take breaks or have a good sleep. Just simply apply this concept to your work and include your daily routine too. Always remember to have a well-balanced diet, keep your body strong by engaging in physical activities and have a good amount of sleep. If you focus on reaching your goals, you must have an understanding of the overall picture. According to the SMART concepts letter T denotes 'time', you should set a period within which you have to try to reach your goal. Well if that is so, tell me where you would get by procrastinating? Believe me, you wouldn't get that far. There is no use in trying to work according to the SMART concept if you have the habit of procrastinating. So what are the benefits and advantages of applying the SMART concept in goal setting?

## 1. Gives you something new to think about

Setting up goals makes you think more individually and creatively. You'll be lighting up a different perspective on things, which helps you consistently achieve your goals.

## 2. Keeps you on the go

Creating a long-term goal can help you motivate yourself

and keep yourself moving forward. The moment your motivation starts to fade, think about how you will feel once you achieve the goals. But remember, motivation is an energy that you can't live without.

## 3. Helps you stay focused

There should be an aim, and it should be achieved. But to achieve an aim, you must have a steady view. If you are not distracted, it will not be a big deal to move towards your goal.

## 4. Supports the timeline

You don't have to adhere to others' timelines when you are achieving your goals. Thus, you can create your own. If you are the one who's creating the timeline, you will be able to decide the time that is required to achieve your goals. But once you set the time, you must not get sidetracked. This way you will be able to manage time without any tightness or tension.

The above mentioned are a few benefits of applying the SMART concept in goal setting. But along with these, there are many more benefits too. The SMART concept is regarded as a promising and successful way to reach your goals. Did you know that there are types of goal setting? You can organize your goal setting in three different ways: short, long,, and lifetime. It doesn't matter whether your goal is short, long, or lifetime, the SMART concept applies to all three types.

You should know that it is perfectly normal not to reach a goal. Do not worry at all. If you are not able to, it happens, and it is not the end of the world. But realize that you need to take action towards your goals. Goals will not magically happen just because you have written them down. Even if you come up with a great SMART plan to achieve your goal, nothing will happen if you do not act on it.

# CHAPTER 13: HOW TO STOP
# OVERTHINKING & NEGATIVE SELF-TALK

One thing that overthinking, worrying, and negative thinking have in common is that they are all mental chatter or mental noise. They are all thoughts that disturb our inner and outer peace. Regardless of the scientific reasons behind them, it is mental noise that becomes embedded in your mind over time. Most times it is uncontrollable - or we think it is uncontrollable - and it often comes out of nowhere when we are in a place mentally and/or physically that we cannot seem to get out of.

However, thoughts and mental chatter can be a good thing when used for productive things, like planning, studying, and analyzing. It's when the thoughts don't have an off-switch that makes it hard to fall or stay asleep and intensifies stress, worry, anger, or other uncomfortable feelings.

Here is a recap of what these mental chatter noises are and how to identify them:

• Negative thoughts or consistent worries that become repetitive;

• Reliving or repetitive images or "movies" that revolve around past experiences or fears;

• Fretting about the past or fearing the unknown uncertainties, distracting us from the present moment;

• Unable to focus on conversations in the present because our minds are constantly thinking about too many things, like tasks we need to do

• Constant worry about what people think of us, so we constantly strive for perfection. Our perfections never seem good enough because our mental chatter never allows us to achieve these goals;

• Involuntary thinking and daydreaming. We overanalyze every situation and stress about the things we are unsure about because we fear the future and overthink about what we can't change.

These types of thought-patterns are unhealthy, and this is why we seem tired and exhausted 90% of the time. In this chapter, I will explain how you can discipline your mind into switching this type of mental chatter off. I will teach you how to reboot your mind so that you can rest easier at night and get some silence when you want to relax. One of the main ways to shut off mental noise is to endure, learn, and practice concentration exercises. Just like all the other techniques explained throughout this book, it is not going to happen overnight, but the more you practice the quieter your mind will get, and eventually it will become second-nature to switch your thinking on and off as if it were a switch.

## Calming Your Mind

Calming your mind is a special skill that takes determination, consistency, and patience. The reason why it is beneficial to quiet your mind is because so many benefits come from having peace within yourself. When you find peace on the inside, it will become easier to find peace outside of you in every situation and environment you surround yourself with. The goal behind inner peace and a quiet mind isn't to stop thinking but to surpass the barriers your mind keeps you trapped in. Here are five secrets to finding inner peace and quieting the mind:

## 1. Listen to and watch the mental noise your thoughts bring you

Watch your thoughts without labeling them. If an intrusive, disturbing thought pops up like, "I wish I were good enough," or "I want to hurt myself," then do not judge it or label it as good, bad, scary, threatening, or anything negative. Notice it and allow it to be there. Don't push it away or avoid it. Don't think about where it came from but embrace that it is there. When you do this, it weakens the power your thoughts have over you, and you gain control of yourself and your worries.

## 2. Consciously and purposely challenge your thoughts

This technique revolves around cognitive behavioral therapy. Many psychologists swear by this method because it means that you can control or alter your thoughts to another direction and create new patterns or habits of the way you interact with your thoughts. You take control back by challenging them

Start by asking yourself about your thoughts. So if your thought is that you aren't good enough, then ask yourself where this comes from. Are you jumping to conclusions? Which one of the cognitive distortions does this thought fall under? Next, find the positive. What has happened in your life that you feel you are not good enough? Finding the root of the thought where it's coming from can really give you insight on taking your control back because then you can replace it with the truth.

### 3. Intentionally focus on your breathing

A lot of the time, we get anxious, worried, or set off our "false alarm" triggers because we aren't breathing properly. Close your eyes and focus on where your breath is coming from, your stomach, chest, or nose. Then just practice noticing your breath without changing it. Once you have figured out where your breath is coming from and how you are breathing, then you can focus on taking in deep, long breaths. Count your inhale to five seconds, hold for three seconds, and exhale for five-to-seven seconds. Repeat until you feel calmer, then go back to normal breathing before you open your eyes again.

## 4. Play calming music which relaxes and motivates you

Music is one of the best healers out there. When we can relate to the singer, they become our favorite artist and then we can feel more relaxed knowing that they are singing about what we feel comfortable relating to. If instrumental is more your thing, then just pay attention to the rhythm and the noise it makes. Close your eyes and try to concentrate on the background noises that you may not have noticed before. Try to name the instruments and memorize the tune.

## 5. Participate in regular exercise

When we exercise on a daily basis, it releases those "feel good" chemicals we previously talked about. When the dopamine is released, it becomes easier for our brain to produce more serotonin which makes us happy. When we are happy, we don't feel so stressed, and our thoughts don't become so overwhelming or overpowering. The idea is to work our bodies physically, so our minds don't have the energy to overthink or create mental chatter.

When we overthink, worry excessively, or think negatively all the time, mental chatter becomes worse, and it can seem impossible to fix. In this next section, I will discuss techniques on how to reboot your brain.

## Brain Reboot

The best way to overcome negative thinking, worrying, and overthinking is to reset the brain. First, you need to be able to accept change and overcome your fears that the thoughts bring into your mind. Secondly, you need to be willing to learn how to change your state of mind and the way you think. So the biggest question is: How do we do this? Most of the "rebooting" process is what we have already talked about. However, the objective of the other techniques was to stop the overthinking patterns. Now, the primary reason most people have an overactive mind is that there is a lot more information to process in today's society compared to three decades ago. Today, we have social networking, technology, and loads of new information that we are interpreting and interacting with daily.

When you read these next techniques on how to reboot your brain, think about the objective as you are learning how to reset the mind, not on how to stop or lessen your thoughts.

## 1. Stop multitasking

Although multitasking can be a good thing, this is one reason why our brain operates on overdrive. When we try to focus, think about, or do too many things at once, it means that our brains are switching focus from one thing to the next, then to the next. This way of thinking actually weakens the ability to get multiple things done at once. For example, do you find when you clean your house that you start with the dishes, then you move on to vacuuming before the dishes are done, then you continue to wipe the counters and find yourself sweeping or mopping the floor twice? You may find that after all that work, you are more exhausted, but when you look around you still have laundry or more dishes to do, and it looks as if you did nothing This is the effect of multitasking.

Multitasking creates shorter attention spans and a distracted mind, also known as the "monkey brain" or the "squirrel effect." To stop multitasking, try focusing on one thing at a time and make sure that you do not move on to the next thing until that one task is completed.

## 2. Concentrate on a single thing at a time

The author of the book called *The Organized Mind: Thinking Straight in the Age of Information Overload,* Daniel Levitin, promotes Deliberate Immersion. Deliberate Immersion means that we split our tasks or duties into time-slots of no more than 30-50 minutes at a time without other distractions. Daniel Levitin says that there are two modes of attention that our brains compose of: The task-positive and the task-negative networks. The task-positive network is the ability to complete tasks without distractions from the outside world or the environment around you, like television, conversations with people that you love in the home, or your phone going off distracting you with social media and what's going on outside the home.

The negative-task network is when your mind is actively daydreaming or wandering, not focusing on the task at hand. It means that you are busy thinking about other things while you are trying to complete a chore. The negative-task network is where creativity and inspiration stem from. Then, we have an "attention filter," which is responsible for switching between the two modes. It helps us stay organized and lets us keep the focus on the current mode we are in, allowing us to complete the given chore we are doing.

### 3. "Attention Filter"

In short to what Daniel Levitin says, is that if you want to be more creatively productive, then you should set aside a time for your social tasks when you are trying to complete a focused or attentive task. This means that there is always a time and place for things like status updates, Twitter, text messages, where you left your wallet, or how to reconcile an argument with a spouse or friend.

When you set aside social aspects to a designated time-period of the day, you will be less distracted and get more things done, which is a great way to reboot the brain when you focus on just ONE thing. The time for task-negative networking (daydreaming and mind wandering or deep thinking) is when you go on nature walks, listen to music while checking social statuses, and bathing with aromatherapy while possibly reading a book.

When we implement mind wandering with these activities, it actually resets our brains and provides different and healthier perspectives on what we are doing or going to do.

## The Four Steps to Mindfulness

Mindfulness is a great method to resetting the brain in the moment. So when you find yourself having "squirrel" moments or have a difficult time in turning off the "monkey mind," return to mindfulness. Mindfulness helps with deeper relaxation techniques - much like meditation, sleep, and concentration.

So, here are the four steps to practicing mindfulness effectively:

### Relabel

Relabeling consists of stepping back and addressing the thought, feeling, or behavior. Ask yourself which cognitive distortion does this thought fall under? Which feeling can you attach this thought to? What does this thought and feeling make you want to do? Why? When you identify these messages, you will be able to better understand where they come from and be able to tell when they are "false alarms."

### Reattribute

Once you have completed identifying the message your thought, feeling, or behavior brings to the surface, you must reassign the thought to a different perspective. Figure out how important the thought is. If it is important or repetitive, then add a new definition behind it and see it in a different light.

## Refocus

Once you have addressed the thought, picked it apart, added meaning, and changed your perception, switch your focus. The point of this is to not get stuck thinking about this for too long as that is why your brain becomes overactive and scattered. It is when you intentionally switch your focus to something else that rewires and resets your brain.

## Revalue

Revaluing happens when you have mastered the other three steps. It happens almost instantly over time. Revaluing means you can see thoughts, urges, and impulses for what they are. When you see these things for what they are, you will have reset your brain to configure and place your thoughts in the correct "brain slots." Your brain will automatically be able to decipher whether a thought or message is beneficial or destructive.

To recap, the easiest way to reboot the brain is to stop multitasking, notice when you are processing or taking on too many tasks or too much information, switch thinking about things to healthy distractions, be mindful of your thoughts, and practice focusing your attention to one thing at a time.

## Analysis Paralysis

"Analysis paralysis or paralysis by analysis is an anti-pattern, the state of over-analyzing (or overthinking) a situation so that a decision or action is never taken, in effect paralyzing the outcome." [1]

I like to think of this in relation to the "flight, fight, freeze" response - analysis paralysis being the freeze reaction. This is when a person gets so caught up in their own thoughts about what to do with a solution to a problem that they can't figure out which solution to choose, so instead they do nothing. Analysis paralysis stems from decision-making skills. American psychologist, Herbert Simon, says that we make decisions in one of two ways:

**Satisfice**

This means that people pick one option that best suits their needs or attention.

**Maximize**

This means that people cannot be satisfied with one decision but make up multiple solutions and always think there are better alternatives than their original decision.

Maximizers are the ones who suffer with analysis paralysis the most. People overthink because they fear their potential mistakes and they avoid the possibility of failure. Analysis paralysis is a fancy word for overthinking combined with the inability to make decisions.

### *Overcoming Analysis Paralysis*

Since analysis paralysis stems from the inability to make

effective and quick decisions, the ways to overcome it is to simply work on your decision-making skills. So here are ways to get unstuck when you have developed overthinking to the point of analysis paralysis:

## 1. Prioritize your decisions

Break your decisions into categories, meaning figure out which decisions are big, and which are small. Which are important, and which decisions don't need much attention. When figuring out which decision to put into which category, ask yourself these questions:

• How important is this decision?

• How immediate is the decision I need to make?

• Is this decision going to make a big or small impact on what happens next?

• What are the best-case and worst-case scenarios based on the solutions I have come up with?

When we categorize our decisions, it makes it easier to stick to our final decision without changing our minds later.

## 2. Find the "end goal" as part of your solution

When you are stuck wondering why you need to make a decision, you can get stuck in the analysis-paralysis trap. Our decisions can revolve around many other thoughts, like "What if I make the wrong choice?" or, "There are so many things I can do, but which is the right decision to make?" If not knowing why you need to make a decision is the case for you, then defining the goal or objective may be a better way to look at the decision that you need to make. For example, imagine you are stuck between choosing between two jobs, you already have a career your succeeding in, but you want something new and are unsure why you need to make a decision or even if you should. Ask yourself what the objective is - where do you envision you should or will be five-to-ten years from now? When you look at the "end goal," it may become easier to figure out what you need to do.

## 3. Break decisions into smaller portions

This technique is like the opposite of the last technique. You are still looking at the "end goal," but instead of making a decision based on the end goal, you are breaking your end goal into a smaller goal. Then you can break your decisions into smaller decisions to complete the "mini goals." While this is still decision making, make sure that when you come to a final decision, you stick with it. If you are still having a hard time deciding, then write your decisions down on paper and come up with no more than three-to-five decisions. Eventually, the more you do this the list will become smaller every time and you will only make one decision. Which is a goal inside itself - to overcome analysis paralysis.

## 4. Get a second opinion

If you are still stuck after you have made your list and you are still overthinking about the many things you can do, then pick two top-solutions and bring them up to a trustee.

In doing this, let go of all judgements within yourself. Let go of control and perfectionism. Rely solely on this other person's opinion, and if they give you advice on a decision you are still unsure about or may not have chosen in the end, then remind yourself that you came to them because you were struggling, and you trust them. Ask yourself how many times this person may have been right when you went against them. Also, tell yourself that you need to let go of the fear that something bad will happen. A quote that has made a big impact for me and people in my life is this: *"Insanity: doing the same thing over and over again and expecting different results."*.[2] So in other words, if you continue to do the same thing but you're expecting something different, then the change will never happen.

**Fear**

A big part of this book says that overthinking, worrying, and negative thinking all revolve around one thing: Fear. Fear of losing control, fear of making a mistake or failing, fear of making a decision, or just a general fear. Fear is learned and can be solved with self-discipline and exposure therapy. Fear is paralyzing and can actually stop someone from doing what they want and make people miss out on successful opportunities. Fear is the number one response to excessive worries and overthinking brains. In order to feel completely in control of our thoughts and actions, it is best to overcome our fears.

Here are some techniques to overcoming fear:

## 1. Acknowledge that the fear (no matter how big or small) is real

When people have fear or are anxious about a specific thing or a variety of things, the fear is real for them. Fear is often a good thing to have; it means that our human instincts are working properly. For example, a woman who is walking home after work in the dark by herself should have worries or fears about walking alone in the dark. A child's first day of school can be worrisome and fearful as well as a child or student who enters a new school in the middle of the year. A man that has to go into surgery on their brain or another functioning organ or someone who needs to go to the dentist both fear the potential for a bad outcome. These are all fears that **should** be there. However, a fear of clowns, small spaces, flying, or heights are all irrational fears or fears that have been learned. Whatever someone fears is real to them and should be looked at with appreciation and never forced to overcome. Fears cannot be overcome unless the person is willing to tackle them.

## 2. Accept your fear

Accept that you have this fear. This could be as big as starting a new job, meeting new people, moving to a new town or city, or becoming a parent. Or it could be as small as a spider that scurries across your feet, weird creaking noises in your new house, someone scaring you, or driving. Whatever it is that makes you fearful, accept that this is the fear you have, don't ignore it, avoid it, or deny it. It's there and you fear it.

## 3. Break it down

Gain some perspective on your fear. Ask yourself:

• What risk are you at?

• Can having this fear really hurt you?

• If your fear came true, then what would happen?

• What is the best-case and the worst-case scenario if this fear were to be right in front of you right now?

Sometimes fears are irrational and cause many people to overthink. Other times overthinking causes new fears to evolve. So once you have asked yourself those questions, ask some more:

• If the scenario happened (worst case) what could you do about it?

• Do you underestimate your ability to handle the situation?

• If the scenario happened (best case) what could you do about it?

• Do you overestimate your ability to handle the situation?

Often times people share the same fears. So find someone who you can share your fears with and strive to overcome them together. When you share the same fears as someone else, you feel a sense of belonging as you are not alone in these fears.

## 4. Give into the fear - assuming the worst

The best way to overcome your fears is to face them or to mindfully pay attention to them. For a while I had anxiety about going out in public. So when I was faced with a public situation, like grocery shopping, I would become overwhelmed and the physical symptoms of fear would kick in - much like a panic attack. When I intentionally went out in public, I first watched my thoughts, and if they were negative, then I would challenge them and replace them with better ones. When my fear became overwhelming, I would go home, but I would try again when I had calmed down - usually the next day. I didn't let fear take control because I kept fighting back. This is also called exposure therapy.

# CHAPTER 14: COMMON PROBLEMS RELATED TO PROCRASTINATION

By now we are completely aware of procrastination. Nobody can say that they don't know about procrastination because they would have experienced it at some point. Some people tend to identify the problem of procrastination, and they eventually treat it. But some others don't! They need support and ideas to overcome procrastination, and it is not something to be ashamed of. It is okay to ask for help and guidance. But the ones who are delayed in identifying procrastination face a lot of problems because of it. If you feel like you are procrastinating, make sure to take the necessary steps to overcome the problem. Don't wait until the last minute to treat it because it is dangerous. However, let us discuss some of the major problems related to procrastination. Here we go:

## *Losing precious time*

If you have heard motivational videos made by Jay Shetty, you'll know how important time is! We waste time as if it doesn't have value, but it is the most valuable thing in the world. If you think about the time you wasted, you will not feel good about yourself. The worst part is when you realize that you've grown up so much, yet you have not changed a bit or even improved at all. You are still in the same place as you were. When this hits you hard, you will not be able to move, and you'll be frozen in the spot wherever you are! I understand it can create terrible feelings. You might regret it, but you can't take back the time that you have misspent.

But it is okay, and it is never too late. You can start now. You can change it now! Think about the changes that you must incorporate and keep following them!

### *Avoiding opportunities*

You might have gotten many opportunities, yet you put off them for tomorrow. The most common word among procrastinators is tomorrow. But little do they know that it is causing so many destructions. When you realize that you have missed so many great opportunities, you might want to slap yourself as hard as you can. But what's the point?

Remember, you are still getting opportunities. Yes, you have got the opportunity to change, so make use of it!

### *Not meeting goals*

This is going to thump you, imagine how long you have been missing your goals. You might have had a strong need to achieve the goals, but then, procrastination happened. When you think about it now, you might feel the deep-cut pain in your chest. But you can still achieve your goals. You just have to uncover the reasons for procrastination and then, get rid of them.

### Missing the ONLY job

You may not have missed out on your job, but some people have missed out or lost their job because of procrastination. Perhaps procrastination is not a trait that employers want to see in employees because it will be a threat to the company's performance. Missing deadlines often and not attending meetings are not great things! You shouldn't procrastinate, it doesn't matter whether it is work or home.

### Lowering self-esteem

Low self-esteem can be one of the reasons why people procrastinate. But the sad part is that your self-esteem goes down even more, when you put off work. You start questioning your capabilities. Moreover, you will lose confidence in yourself and become vulnerable. Low self-esteem is a significant threat to your life, so find solutions to overcome this problem.

### Poor decision-making

When you become a pro at procrastination, you become a novice at decision-making. When you procrastinate, your decisions will be based on the things that you believe are right. Your emotions will take a toll on you at this point.

Eventually, poor decision-making will make your life miserable.

### Damaged reputation

If you don't do something that you haven't promised, it is okay. But when you say something that you will never do, it is going to be dangerous. For example, you keep missing the deadlines and give great excuses. How far can you take this lie? Do you think you will still have the job after missing too many deadlines? The client may have a bad impression of your reputation. In this case, through procrastination, you are damaging your reputation as well. You will see that people stop sending you tasks or people stop contacting you for important work because they know you are not the right person. You will always be considered as someone who'll not be able to complete a task in a given time. A damaged reputation is never easy to handle.

### Risking your health

Another common problem associated with procrastination is that of stress, fear, anxiety, and many other health issues. If you think health issues related to procrastination ONLY concern your mental health, well, I'm sorry to say that there's more to it. Even though mental health issues are also severe, you will end up hurting your overall body by procrastinating. Like we discussed earlier, there are chances for you to get different types of diseases if you don't work accordingly. Basically, due to procrastination, you tend to work day and night without actually giving enough importance to your body. Do you really know how vulnerable your body is? Do you know how carefully you should handle your body? If you know all these, you wouldn't even think of procrastination. Typically, procrastinators don't spend much time analyzing these things. Instead, they do their job —wasting time!

### Sacrificing your happiness

You will not understand the factor of sacrificing happiness until reality hits you hard. You might often be procrastinating, but you get the work done in the minute, and that makes you think that you can are capable of doing something when you want to do it. There is a clear-cut difference between determination and procrastination. Determination is when you don't delay the work for the second time. Basically, by completing the work at the last moment, you are losing a lot of things. For example, if there is a family event planned, you will not be able to attend it because you are too busy working. Likewise, you might sacrifice your happiness whenever you procrastinate. Procrastination is not only unhealthy but also makes you unhappy!

These are just some of the common problems related to procrastination, but there are many other severe problems. You are lucky, you have decided to change, and that's why you have reached the last page of this book. I hope you change for the better and have a productive life!

# CONCLUSION

It is easy to get distracted, but it takes a lot of practice to avoid distractions. Recently, I watched one of the motivational videos made by Jay Shetty, and as he clearly mentions you must not run away from distractions.[1] Instead, you must master the art of avoiding them. Simply shutting down your phone or not opening a tab for Facebook login, will not help you become productive. To become productive and to overcome procrastination, you must ensure to tame your mind.

Even if there are distractions, you must be able to focus on the important things. If you know how to differentiate important tasks and trivial tasks, you'll easily overcome procrastination. But the difficulty is in taming your mind. For this, we've discussed many practical tips and exercises for you to follow.

Sometimes, by the time you understand the influence caused

by procrastination, it will be too late to correct things. In life, you have to seize the chances that you get because it only takes a few seconds before it reaches another person.

If you know the importance of time, you will not waste it. Most of us do not value time, and if you start looking at a time like your hard-earned money, you'll think twice before spending it unnecessarily. Do you spend your hard-earned money unnecessarily? You don't because you know how HARD you worked to earn it.

The only difference between time and money is that you earn money and you get time. Nobody earns time, so it is hardly considered important. If you look at time as if looking at money, you'll spend it wisely. Think about this, and it will sound so practical that you might start thinking twice before you switch on the TV while you have a project to submit.

However, if you are a procrastinator and you'd love to change yourself, it might take some time because it is not easy to change all of a sudden. Then again, if you change within a short time, it is going to be beneficial for you.

"Only put off until tomorrow what you are willing to die having left undone"[2] — Pablo Picasso

If this makes sense, you will not put off things for tomorrow. I genuinely hope «How to stop procrastinating» has been a book worth reading.

Thank you for reading!

# SOME BOOKS YOU MAY FIND INTERESTING

## How to Stop Overthinking

*The 7-Step Plan to Control and Eliminate Negative Thoughts, Declutter Your Mind and Start Thinking Positively in 5 Minutes or Less*

Do you find yourself lying awake at night because you can't stop worrying about what happened today? Are you constantly second-guessing almost every decision that you are faced with in life? Do your job, friendships or whole life seem to be overwhelming?

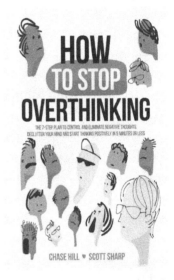

By reading this book, you will emboldened yourself to deal with your fears, anxiety, handle your perfectionism, and stop your overthinking for good.

What you should expect along the journey of practicing the techniques and strategies throughout this book is to be aware of where your mental chatter comes from, and how to address it.

Stop worrying about what you did today and start living in

the moment. Stop living for tomorrow and start breathing in the positivity of today. Stop overthinking your future and make big changes to live your future now.

We are only ever promised today, so instead of obsessing over what you could have done at that social event or trying to control what you will do in your next appointment, learn to breathe in this moment you have now.

What you'll learn

• How to Control Overthinking and Eliminate Negative Thoughts in Just a Few Minutes.

• 10 Powerful Tactics to Stop Anxiety and Worrying Permanently.

• How to Sleep Better, Even if Your Head Is Full of Thoughts.

• Simple Tips to Develop Self-Confidence and Decision-Making Skills.

• How to Remove Toxicity and Change Your Relationships for the Better.

• 5 Ways to Calm Anxiety (Worrying) in Five Minutes or Less.

• Troubleshooting Guide if Nothing Helps.

• How to Declutter Your Mind and Become What You Want in Life.

This book will go through the reasons why the way you think now is not beneficial to your being and how positivity can greatly improve your outlook and put yourself in the direction you want your life to go.

So, quit being stuck, stop letting your mind trap you, and take control of what you want. There are finally lessons and a structure to get you to where you **want** to be rather than where you are now. AND, it's all in this book.

**Would You Like To Know More?**

Download this book to get started and turn off your over-thinking for good!

Scan the QR code below to get it immediately.

## Mind Hacking Secrets

*21 Neuroscience Ways to Develop Fast, Clear & Critical Thinking. Learn How to Train Your Brain to Think Faster and Clearly in 2 Weeks.*

Do you long to be able to have clear thinking, a clear mind, organizational skills, and the ability to recall information more efficiently? Are there moments when you wish you could learn faster, remember more, and be more productive?

Your brain is an incredible tool that will never fail to amaze even the most talented scientists out there, but...

The problem is that it isn't thinking in the way that you want it to. You can get hung up on small details, become easily distracted, and forget important information that you want to remember.

The solution to your biggest neuroscience issues lies within your head. There is no pill, surgery, or another quick method that is going to give you a new way of thinking. All the changes that you wish to make within your neurology are entirely possible by using your brain!

We are going to give you actionable steps to help you get the results you want.

This book is going to be a practical guide for you to improve the way that you think overall. The purpose of this reading will be to provide you with foundational "how-to" knowledge so you can apply what you learn to your life to see instant results.

We will teach you how to think fast, clearly, and critically. We will help you improve your focus, reasoning, judgment, analysis, and ability to make certain choices. We will help you increase your writing skills, as well as your ability to speak.

You will understand how to keep your brain sharp through critical thinking, improved decision-making skills, and problem-solving abilities. When you practice applying these methods and practical tips that are discussed throughout this book, you are unlocking your greatest potential.

**What you'll learn:**

• How to Be More Productive and Do More in a Less Time.

• 21 Neuroscience Ways to Develop Fast, Clear and Critical Thinking.

• How to Hack Your Way to a Sharper, Smarter, and More Resilient Brain.

• Powerful Methods for Developing Critical Thinking and Avoiding Manipulation Tactics

• Action Plan for How to Train Your Brain to Think Faster in 2 Weeks

We will provide you with all that is needed to unlock the secrets of your mind. This is a must-read for anyone that wants to know how they can get the things they desire most with the full use of their brain.

**Would you like to know more?**

Get your copy now and start training!

## Unlimited Memory Power

*How to Remember More, Improve Your Concentration and Develop a Photographic Memory in 2 Weeks.*

Do you want to have a better memory? Do you want to boost your brain so you can learn faster, remember more, and be more productive?

Perhaps you want to have a photographic memory and want to be a superhero who can remember all kinds of information, including details of facts, people's names, and events...

We have everything you need in this book, *Unlimited Memory Power*. As you read, you will learn actionable steps to get the results you want by improving memory and boosting your memory's capacity. You will discover how to train your brain to remember more and learn faster, using special memory improvement exercises.

This book presents a plan to train your memory with a challenge for your mind, body, and soul. We offer a total package — diet, exercise, stress relief, and memory tricks to help you remember.

In this book, you will learn basic skills and more advanced strategies, including mnemonic devices, the memory palace, the military method, and much more.

You will train a photographic memory that enables you to remember faces and names, numbers, dates, foreign languages, and even game cards. I will also show you how to improve your reading skills. Also, we will talk about the foods that contribute to your memory.

**What you'll learn:**

• Advanced Learning Strategies to Remember More in Less Time.

• How Memorize Names, Dates, Game Cards and Useful Info Like a Superhero.

• The Main Secret of Better Focus and Concentration.

• High-Speed Memory Tips.

• A Brain-Enhancing and Memory Improvement Menu.

• An Action Plan for How to Improve Memory in Two Weeks.

• Foreign Language Hacking - The Best Methods to Learn and Speak a New Language.

• The Beginner's Guide to Developing Photographic Memory Skills.

**+ BONUS: 21 Memory Improvement Exercises and Techniques**

You will see you some real-life examples, case studies that illustrate how people put into practice the points explained, with excellent results. These scenarios will give you a clear idea of how to apply the methods we have talked about in this book. To protect the privacy of the individuals, we have chosen to introduce alternate names.

We invite you to come on this journey to enhance your brainpower. You will discover how exciting it is to develop your memory and increase your concentration. Then, you can truly be the most successful and fulfilled version of yourself.

**Read on to find out further about how you can remember more, stress less, and enjoy a meaningful and productive life starting right now!**

# NOTES

## Chapter 2: How to Reduce Procrastination Easily

1. Michael Korda Quotes. (2019)

## Chapter 3: Best Anti-Procrastination Equipment

1. https://www.merriam-webster.com/dictionary/kamikaze

## Chapter 8: How to Use Gamification to Stop Procrastinating

1. Games and Your Brain: How to Use Gamification to Stop Procrastinating. (2013).
2. Lifehacker.com (2019)

## Chapter 11: The Power of Willpower

1. Big Think. (2013)
2. Sleep Needs. (2018)

## Chapter 13: How to Stop Overthinking & Negative Self-Talk

1. https://community.uservoice.com/blog/analysis-paralysis-what-it-is-and-how-to-avoid-it/

ps://www.brainyquote.com/quotes/unknown_133991

## Conclusion

1. Jay Shetty, 2018
2. Procrastination Quotes, 2019

# REFERENCES

Barnes, Z. (2019). 11 Ways To Finally Stop Procrastinating And Get Stuff Done. SELF. Retrieved 24 April 2019, from https://www.self.com/story/11-ways-to-finally-stop-procrastinating-and-get-stuff-done

Definition of KAMIKAZE. (2019). Merriam-webster.com. Retrieved 24 April 2019, from https://www.merriam-webster.com/dictionary/kamikaze

Games and Your Brain: How to Use Gamification to Stop Procrastinating. (2013). Resources. Retrieved 27 April 2019, from https://buffer.com/resources/brain-playing-games-why-our-brains-are-so-attracted-to-playing-games-the-science-of-gamification

Hennekes, B. (2018). 6 Proven Ways To Reduce Procrastina-

Pavlok. Pavlok. Retrieved 24 April 2019, from ps://pavlok.com/blog/procrastination/

Introduction to Goal Setting. (2019). Goalscape. Retrieved 24 April 2019, from https://goalscape.com/en/blog/introduction-goal-setting/

Jay Shetty. (2018, September 27). *If you need to focus-watch this* [Video File]. Retrieved from https://www.youtube.com/watch?v=KawmQolLaUM

Kirstin O'Donovan. (2018) 8 Dreadful Effects of Procrastination That Can Destroy Your Life. (2014). Lifehack. Retrieved 24 April 2019, from https://www.lifehack.org/articles/productivity/8-ways-procrastination-can-destroy-your-life.html

Lifehacker.com. (2019). Retrieved 27 April 2019, from https://lifehacker.com/beat-procrastination-with-temptation-bundling-1781175382

Michael Korda Quotes. (2019). BrainyQuote. Retrieved 24 April 2019, from https://www.brainyquote.com/quotes/michael_korda_135023

Problems With Procrastination. (2017). The Odyssey Online. Retrieved 24 April 2019, from https://www.theodysseyonline.com/problems-procrastination

Procrastination Quotes (2019) (414 quotes). Goodreads.com. Retrieved 17 April 2019, from https://www.goodreads.com/quotes/tag/procrastination

Sleep Needs. (2018). HelpGuide.org. Retrieved 27 April 2019, from https://www.helpguide.org/articles/sleep/sleep-needs-get-the-sleep-you-need.htm/

The Difference Between "I Can't" And "I Don't". (2019). Big Think. Retrieved 27 April 2019, from https://bigthink.com/ideafeed/the-difference-between-i-cant-and-i-dont

Waitley, D. (2016). 9 Ways to Stop Procrastinating and Get Things Done. SUCCESS. Retrieved 24 April 2019, from https://www.success.com/9-ways-to-stop-procrastinating-and-get-things-done

YourCoach Gent. (2019) S.M.A.R.T. goal setting | SMART | Coaching tools | Yourcoach.be. Retrieved 24 April 2019, from https://www.yourcoach.be/en/coaching-tools/smart-goal-setting.php